Henry Harrison

The Place-Names of the Liverpool District

The history and meaning of the local and river names of South-west

Lancashire and of Wirral

Henry Harrison

The Place-Names of the Liverpool District
The history and meaning of the local and river names of South-west Lancashire and of Wirral

ISBN/EAN: 9783337234423

Printed in Europe, USA, Canada, Australia, Japan

Cover: Foto ©Andreas Hilbeck / pixelio.de

More available books at **www.hansebooks.com**

'*Liverpool . . . that Saxon hive.*'—MATTHEW ARNOLD.

'*Liverpool . . . the greatest commercial city in the world.*'
NATHANIEL HAWTHORNE.

'*That's a great city, and those are the lamps. It's Liverpool.*'
'Christopher Tadpole' (A. SMITH).

'*In the United Kingdom there is no city which from early days has inspired me with so much interest, none which I would so gladly serve in any capacity, however humble, as the city of Liverpool.*'
REV. J. E. C. WELLDON.

THE PLACE-NAMES OF THE LIVERPOOL DISTRICT;

OR,

The History and Meaning of the Local and River Names of South-west Lancashire and of Wirral.

BY

HENRY HARRISON.

'RESPICIENDUM EST UT DISCAMUS EX PRÆTERITO.'

LONDON:
ELLIOT STOCK, 62, PATERNOSTER ROW, E.C.
1898.

To

SIR JOHN T. BRUNNER, BART.,

OF "DRUIDS' CROSS," WAVERTREE,

MEMBER OF PARLIAMENT FOR THE NORTHWICH

DIVISION OF CHESHIRE,

THIS LITTLE VOLUME IS RESPECTFULLY DEDICATED

BY HIS OBEDIENT SERVANT,

THE AUTHOR.

CONTENTS.

	PAGE
INTRODUCTION	5
BRIEF GLOSSARY OF SOME OF THE CHIEF ENGLISH PLACE-NAME COMPONENTS	17
DOMESDAY ENTRIES	20
LINGUISTIC ABBREVIATIONS, ETC.	23
LIVERPOOL	24
HUNDRED OF WEST DERBY	33
HUNDRED OF WIRRAL	75
LIST OF WORKS QUOTED	101

INTRODUCTION.

This little onomasticon embodies, I believe, the first attempt to treat the etymology of the place-names of the Liverpool district upon a systematic basis. In various local and county histories endeavours have here and there been made to account for the origin of certain place-names, but such endeavours have unfortunately only too frequently been remarkable for anything but philological, and even topographical, accuracy. They are, however, generally chronicled, as a matter of record, in the present monograph, with such criticism and emendation as may have been thought necessary.

The science of philology has made rapid strides since the days when Syers, in his *History of Everton*, solemnly asserted that etymology, a branch of philology, was neither more nor less than "guessology"; but even to-day, after all the accessible historical and philological evidence bearing upon a name has been thoroughly sifted and carefully weighed, there sometimes remains an element of uncertainty that creates a hiatus which must be filled by guessing—but, still, by what Professor Skeat has called, in this connection, "reasonable guessing,"[1] not the kind of etymo-

---

[1] Dr. Sweet says, in the preface to his new Anglo-Saxon Dictionary: 'The investigator of Old English . . . is often obliged to work by guesswork, until some one else guesses better."

logical jumping at conclusions which has, for example, induced a Welshman to claim that the name Apollo is derived from the Cymric *Ap-haul*, 'Son of the Sun'; an Irishman to assert that the Egyptian deity Osiris was of Hibernian descent, and that the name should consequently be written O'Siris; a Cornishman, saturated with the Phœnician tradition, to declare that his Honeyball is a corruption of Hannibal; a Scotsman to infer an affinity between the Egyptian Pharaoh and the Gaelic Fergus; and even an Englishman to calmly asseverate that Lambeth (the 'lamb-hithe'), containing the palace of the Archbishop of Canterbury, derived its name from the Thibetan *llama*, 'high-priest,' and the Hebrew *beth*, 'house.'

While, however, in England, we bring our guessing powers into operation only, as a rule, after the lapse of centuries, in America it sometimes happens that a place receives its name one day and the next (so to speak) the origin of that name is shrouded in mystery, as witness the following characteristic extract from a recent number of a Western States journal:

"Nobody around the oilfields seems to know why the new field is called Chipmunk. Most aver that it has always been Chipmunk ever since the time of the mound-builders. Others have it that the first white settler was eaten by chipmunks, ever since which notable event a pure white chipmunk has haunted the valley, scaring other chipmunks to death. Chipmunk may also be called Chipmunk because there are no chipmunks there."

In order to impose a more or less recognised limit upon the so-called district of Liverpool, it has, for the purpose of this treatise, been divided into two hundreds—that of West Derby, which comprises practically the whole of south-west Lancashire, and that of Wirral, which embraces the tongue of land separating the estuary of the Mersey from that of the Dee. The names enumerated in the body of the work, which is arranged in alphabetical form with respect to the two hundreds, I have summarized herewith, according to their linguistic origin:

HUNDRED OF WEST DERBY.

Anglo-Saxon.	Norse.	Celtic. Gaelic.	Celtic. Cymric.	Anglo-Saxon or Norse.	English and Arbitrary.	Norman-French.	Hybrid and Doubtful.
Abram.							
Aigburth.							
Aintree.							
Allerton.							
Arbury.							
Atherton.							
Aughton.							
Bamfurlong.							
Barton.							
Bedford.							
Billinge.							
Bold.							
Bootle.							
Burtonwood.							
Chowbent.							
Croft.							
Cronton.							
Cuerdley.							
Dallum.							
Dalton.							
Ditton.							
Downholland.							
Eccleston.							
Everton.							
Farnworth.							
Fazakerley.							
Fearnhead.							
Garston.	Pennington.						
Gateacre.	Poulton.						
Golborne.	Prescot.						
Haigh.	Rainford.						
Hale.	Risley.						
Halsall.	Rixton.						
Haydock.	Sankey.						
Hindley.	Southworth.						
Hollinfare.	Speke.						
Houghton.	Spellow.						
Hulme.	Stanley.						
Huyton.	Thornton.						
Knowsley.	Toxteth.						
Leigh.	Tuebrook.						
Linacre.	Tyldesley.						
Lowton.	Upholland.						
Lydiate.	Walton.						
Makerfield.	Wargrave.						
Mersey (r.).	Warrington.						
Netherton.	Wavertree.						
Newsham.	Whiston.						
Newton.	Wigan.						
Orford.	Windle.						
Padgate.	Winstanley.						
Parr.	Winwick.						
Pemberton.	Woolston.						
Penketh.	Woolton.						
	Liverpool.	Alt (r.).	Bryn.				
	Bickerstaffe.	Douglas (r.).	Melling.				
	Burscough.	Glaze[brook] (r.).	Kenyon.				
	Childwall.						
	Crosby.						
	Crossens.						
	Croxteth.						
	Formby.			Ainsdale.			Altcar.
	Ince.			Birkdale.			Culcheth.
	Kirkby.			Sephton.			Cunscough.
	Kirkdale.			Maghull.			Glazebrook.
	Lathom.			Rainhill.			
	Litherland.						
	Lunt.				Anfield.		
	North Meols.				Bank Hall.		
	Ormskirk.				Blundellsands.		
	Orrell.				Freshfield.		
	Ravensmeols.				Scaforth (arbit.).		
	Roby.				Southport.		
	Scarisbrick.				St. Helens.		
	Skelmersdale.				Waterloo (arbit.).		
	Tarbock.						
	Thingwall.						
	West Derby.						
	Widnes.						

HUNDRED OF WIRRAL.

Anglo-Saxon.

Backford.
Bebington.
Bilston.
Blacon.
Burton.
Capenhurst.
Childer Thornton.
Chorlton.
Claughton.
Croughton.
Eastham.
Ellesmere.
Gayton.
Greasby.
Hoose.
Hooton.
Hoylake.
Leasowes, The.
Ledsham.
Leighton.
Mollington.
Moreton.
Neston.
Netherpool.
Overchurch.
Overpool.
Oxton.
Poolton.
Poulton Lancelyn.
Prenton.
Puddington.
Saughall.
Seacombe.
Soughall.
Stanney.
Stoke.
Storeton.
Sutton.
Thornton Hough.
Upton.
Willaston.
Wirral.

Norse.

Brimstage.
Caldy.
Frankby.
Heswall.
Hilbre.
Irby.
Meols.
Pensby.
Raby.
Thingwall.
Thurstaston.
West Kirkby.
Whitby.

Anglo-Saxon or Norse.

Barnston.
Birkenhead.
Bromborough.
Hargrave.
Larton.
Ness.
Shotwick.
Wallasey.

Celtic.

Gaelic.

Landican.
Liscard.
Noctorum.

Cymric.

Arrowe.
Dee (r.).
Gowy (r.).
Tranmere.

Norman-French.

Spital.

English and Arbitrary.

Egremont (arbit.).
Fender (r.).
New Brighton (arbit.).
Parkgate.

Latino-Saxon.

(Chester.)

The chief fact to be gathered from these lists is that both in south-west Lancashire and in Wirral the Anglo-Saxon names are about three times as numerous as those of Norse origin; and it was to be expected that, in a part of the country which was wrested from the British at a later period than is assigned to the Saxon conquest of most of the remaining portions of what ultimately came to be called England, distinct traces of Celtic nomenclature should be met with.[1]

"Letters, like soldiers," that acute philologist Horne Tooke once observed, "are very apt to desert and drop off in a long march." Of this truism the vicinity of Liverpool is not behind other districts in affording good illustrations. The Norse Otegrimele and Otringemele, as chronicled in Domesday, have descended to us in the attenuated form of Orrell; Levetesham is now Ledsham; Stochestede, Toxteth; Chenulveslei, Knowsley; Herleshala, Halsall; and so on. On the other hand, there are names which, in the course of time, have added a trifle to their length. Oxton at one period was Oxon; Speke was Spec.

Luckily we are not blessed—or the reverse—with many names of the "funny" order, or even of that American genus against which Matthew Arnold declaimed: "When our race has built Bold Street, Liverpool, and pronounced it very good," caustically observed the author of *The Study of Celtic Literature* (p. 175), "it hurries across the Atlantic and builds Nashville, and Jacksonville, and Milledgeville,

---

[1] Wordsworth, whose Poems on the Naming of Places will be familiar to the reader, has well expressed in verse the changes wrought in Britain by the Saxon Conquest—
"Another language spreads from coast to coast;
Only perchance some melancholy stream
And some indignant hills old names preserve,
When laws, and creeds, and people all are lost!"—
Monastery of Old Bangor.

and thinks it is fulfilling the designs of Providence in an incomparable manner."

Possibly Arnold may have borne in mind, too, the ludicrous origin of such American place-names as Elberon (L. B. Brown), Carasaljo (Carrie, Sally, and Joe), Eltopia (Hell-to-pay), and Nameless, which last-mentioned town received its incongruous designation because a lazy postal official at Washington, having repeatedly been urged by the inhabitants of a new and thriving village in Laurens County, Georgia, to select a name for it, at last testily telegraphed to the astonished settlers, " Let it remain nameless "; and Nameless accordingly the place has been ever since. But, as I have remarked, we of the Liverpool district have very few of the kind of names at which an American once poked revengeful fun in a set of verses, one of which ran :

> "At Scrooby and at Gonexby,
> At Wigton and at Smeeth,
> At Bottesford and Runcorn,
> I need not grit my teeth ;
> At Swineshead and at Crummock,
> At Sibsey and Spithead,
> Stoke Pogis and Wolsoken,
> I will not wish me dead."

Still we have to confess, with some degree of sadness, to a Puddington, a Mollington, a Noctorum, and a Greasby, all in Wirral; while, as to the Lancashire side of the Mersey, we have often seen and heard prettier and more euphonious names than, say, Ravensmeols, Bold, Maghull, Skelmersdale, and Chowbent. Even a silver-tongued Whitefield, who was reputed to be able to "pronounce 'Mesopotamia' so as to make a congregation weep," would, we should imagine, have experienced some difficulty in investing with charm the utterance of the names which we have just enumerated.

I have compiled (with special reference to the Hundreds of West Derby and Wirral) and appended to the Introduction a brief glossary of some of the most frequently occurring English place-name components. It might perhaps be considered amply sufficient when we recollect the Elizabethan Verstegan's oft misquoted couplet:

"In ford, in ham, in ley, and tun,
 The most of English surnames [place-names] run."
 (*Restitution of Decayed Intelligence in Antiquities.*)

But we must not forget that, as Kemble says (*Cod. Dipl.* iii. xv.), speaking of Anglo-Saxon place-nomenclature: "The distinctions between even the slightest differences in the face of the country are marked with a richness and accuracy of language which will surprise . . ." The components embodied in another well-worn distich:

"By tre, pol, and pen,
 Ye shall know the Cornishmen,"

do not, of course, come within the scope of the glossary.

Mention should be made of the difficulties which the Norman Conquest was the means of strewing, like caltrops or *chevaux-de-frise*, in the path of the investigator of Anglo-Saxon nomenclature. "The Normans," says Skeat, "spelt Anglo-Saxon names anyhow." "The Normans," Kemble grumbled, referring to the terms in Anglo-Saxon charters, "could not even spell the words." "The loose manner of spelling the names of English places in Doomsday Book cannot," observed Gregson in his *Portfolio of Fragments*, "be wondered at when it is considered that the Normans had the chief hand in compiling the returns."

Hardy, in his *Introduction* to the Close Rolls, portions of which essay have been borrowed by the writers of the

Pipe Roll Society's introductory volume as being also applicable to the rolls with which they were dealing, remarks: "Great ambiguity prevails in the proper names of persons and places which occur on the Close Rolls; for these were either Latinized or Gallicized, whenever it was possible to do so, according to the fancy of the scribe or the degree of knowledge which he happened to possess. Thus he rendered into Latin or French a Norman or Saxon appellation just as he happened to prefer the one to the other.... Whitchurch is sometimes written De Albo Monasterio, sometimes Blancmuster or Blauncmustier."

Mr. G. Grazebrook, in a paper read before the Society of Antiquaries in February, 1897, on the spelling of mediæval names, submitted a list of sixty-one various forms in which the name Grazebrook is found from the year 1200.

A good instance of the vagaries of a Norman writer or copyist of Anglo-Saxon is supplied in a MS. of 'The Proverbs of Alfred,' upon which Professor Skeat read a paper in May, 1897, at a meeting of the Philological Society (*Athenæum*, May 15, '97). The Norman scribe who wrote out this MS. has, amongst other blunders and peculiarities, *t*, and occasionally *d*, for final *th*, and, conversely, *th* for the English final *t*; *st* (with long *s*) for the final *ght*; *s* for *sh*, as *sal* for *shal*; *w* for *wh*, as *wat* for *what*; *cherril* for *churl*; *arren* for *arn*; *welethe* for *welthe*; *chil* for *child*; *wen* for *went*; *kinc* for *king*; *wrsipe* for *worship*; *hunt* for *hund*, and *ant* for *and*. And when we find, to carry example a little further, an Anglo-Saxon *Hweorfanhealh* transformed in Domesday into *Vurvenele*, there is little ground for wonder that the pursuit of the etymology of a local name should sometimes be a tedious operation, although it must be said that there is scarcely need to spend the leisure of thirty years in endeavouring to ascertain the origin of a single place-name, as a resident of Kensington recently confessed in *Notes and Queries* to have done.

Of course, many amateur topographical derivation hunters lose considerable time in persistently endeavouring to trace the first element of an English place-name to some physical feature or characteristic, simple or complex, when all the time the prefix is often merely a personal name, possibly somewhat corrupted. It has probably been the fashion in all ages, and in all countries, for personal nomenclature to be used, in greater or less degree, in place designation: " And Cain . . . builded a city, and called the name of the city after the name of his son Enoch."—*Gen.* iv. 17. " And they called the name of the city Dan, after the name of Dan their father."—*Judges* xviii. 29.

For the benefit of the general reader it may not be thought superfluous to state that, of the two State Records of which the most frequent mention is made in the course of the monograph, the immortal Domesday Book was completed in A.D. 1086 ; while the Testa de Nevill, or, to give the Exchequer collection its full title, ' Testa de Nevill, sive Liber Feodorum in Curia Scaccarii,' relates ostensibly, and with little actual variation, to the times of Henry III. and Edward I. (1216 to 1307), and was compiled at the beginning of the reign of Edward III. The collection of Anglo-Saxon charters printed by Kemble—*Codex Diplomaticus Ævi Saxonici*—is comprised in six volumes, the first of which was published in 1839, the last in 1848. This work has now, to some extent, been superseded by the *Cartularium Saxonicum* of Mr. de Gray Birch, the chief continuator of Kemble. The *History of Lancashire* quoted, with the date, for the second volume, of 1870, is Baines's excellent compilation as edited by the late John Harland, F.S.A., and continued and completed by Mr. Brooke Herford; although where necessary reference is made to Croston's edition, 1888-93. Ormerod's monumental *History of Cheshire*, first published in 1819, was reissued in a revised form in 1882 by Mr. Helsby. Mr. Beamont's *Domesday Cheshire and Lancashire* should be mentioned in conjunction with Colonel James's *Domesday Facsimile* of those two counties. The Publications of the Chetham Society, the Record Society of Lancashire and Cheshire (which printed the collection of Lancashire and Cheshire documents in the Public Record Office edited by Mr. W. D. Selby, author of the *vade-mecum* of record searchers, *The Jubilee Date Book*), the Historic Society of Lancashire and Cheshire, the Literary and Philosophical Society of Liverpool, the Lancashire and Cheshire Antiquarian Society, and the Chester Architectural, Archæological, and Historic Society of course provide splendid raw material for the student of Lancashire and Cheshire place-names, although here and there a paper with a not unpromising title, and by a well-known scholar, may, upon investigation, prove to be disappointing, as, for instance, Dr. Latham's essay 'On the Language of Lancashire under the Romans,' in vol. ix. (1857) of the *Transactions* of the Lancashire and Cheshire Historic Society.

My indebtedness for miscellaneous information to the above-mentioned and various other works (including the valuable treatises of the Rev. Canon Taylor), and to local antiquaries, is duly recorded in the proper place, and a bibliography is appended; but I should specially mention some MS. notes which Prof. Skeat, author of the much-used *Etymological Dictionary*, kindly placed at my disposal.

Unfortunately, the aforesaid student of predial names in Lancashire and Cheshire cannot avail himself of a record which the topographic investigator in most other English counties can study with profit, *viz.*, the Rotuli Hundredorum, or Hundred Rolls (*temp.* Hen. III. and Edw. I.), which contain no extract relative to the Counties Palatine of Lancaster and Chester.

BRIEF GLOSSARY OF SOME OF THE CHIEF ENGLISH PLACE-NAME COMPONENTS.

(Compiled with special reference to the Liverpool District.)

AC, ACK, AIG, AIK	A.-Sax. *ác*, oak.
ACRE, A(C)KER	A.-Sax. *æcer*, field, acre.
AS-T	A.-Sax. *eást*, east.
BAR	A.-Sax. *bere*, barley.
BOLD, BOOTLE	A.-Sax. *bold, botl*, dwelling.
BOROUGH, BURGH, BURY	(1) A.-Sax. *burh, burg*, Scand. *borg*, fortified place, castle, city; (2) A.-Sax. *beorh, beorg*, hill.
BUR	A.-Sax. *búr* (boor), one of the lowest class of freemen, a husbandman; also a bower.
BY	O. Nor. *bær. býr* (Dan.-Norw. and Swed. *by*), settlement, farmstead, village.
CARL (Eastern and Northern, *i.e.*, Angl. and Dan.), CHARL (Southern), CHORL (Midland)	A.-Sax. *carl* (Scand. *karl*), *ceorl* (churl), one of the lowest class of freemen, a husbandman. (A slave was a *theów* or a *thræl*, whence the surnames Thew and Thrale).
CASTER (Angl. and Dan.), CESTER, CHESTER } Sax.	Lat. *castra* (pl. of *castrum*), camp; whence A.-Sax. *ceaster*, city.
DAL-E, DEL-L	(1) A-Sax. *dæl*, Scand. *dal*, dale; (2) A.-Sax. *dǽl*, Scand. *del*, deal, allotment.
EA, EY	(1) A.-Sax. *ig* (iy), O. Nor. *ey*, island, low riparian tract; (2) A.-Sax. *eá*, O. Nor. *á*, river.
GARS	A.-Sax. *gærs*, grass.
GAT-E	(1) A.-Sax. *geat*, gate, passage, road; (2) A.-Sax. *gát*, goat.
GRAF (prefix), GRAVE, GREVE	(1) A.-Sax. *gráf*, grove; (2) A.-Sax. *græf*, O. Nor. *gröf* (Dan. *grav*, Swed. *graf*), trench, ditch.
HAL(L)-E	(1) A.-Sax. *healh*, O. Nor. *hall(r)*, slope, hill, corner; (2) A.-Sax. *heall*, hall.
HAM	(1) A.-Sax. *hám*, home; (2) A.-Sax. *ham(m)*, piece of land, often hemmed in by the bend of a river.

HAR	(1) A.-Sax. *hara*, Scand. *hare*, hare (combined with grove, wood, field, ley, etc.); (2) A.-Sax. *hár*, O. Nor. *harr*, grey; (3) O. Nor. *hár*, high; (4) ? A.Sax. *here*, O. Nor. *herr*, military.
HARD	A.-Sax. *heorde*, herd; occasionally A.Sax. personal name *Heard* = brave.
HAIGH HAY	A.-Sax. *hege*, *haga*, hedge, enclosure.
HOGH HOO HOUGH	A.-Sax. *hó*, *hôh*, hough, heel; point of land formed like a heel.
HOLM-E HULME	A.-Sax. and O. Nor. *holm*, river-island, low riparian land.
HOLT	A.-Sax. *holt*, copse, wood.
HURST	A.-Sax. *hyrst*, copse, wood.
ING	A.-Sax. suffix denoting 'son of,' in pl. 'descendants of.'
KIRK	O. Nor. *kirkja* (Dan.-Norw. *kirke*, Swed. *kyrka*), A.-Sax. *circe*, church.
LEA LEE LEY LEIGH	A.-Sax. *leáh*, meadow, pasture.
LOW	A.-Sax. *hlǽw*, (burial) mound, hill.
MEOLS	O. Nor, *mel(r)*, sandhill, sandbank.
NES-S	O. Nor. *nes* (Dan.-Norw. *nes*, Swed. *näs*), A.-Sax. *næss*, headland, promontory.
NETHER	A.-Sax. *neother*, lower.
OVER	(1) A.-Sax. *ofer*, upper; (2) A.-Sax. *ófer*, bank, shore.
POOL POUL	A.-Sax. *pól*, O. Nor. *poll(r)*, pool.
SCOUGH SHAW	O.-Nor. *skógr* (Swed. *skog*, Dan.-Norw. *skov*), A.-Sax. *sceaga*, 'grove,' 'wood.'
SHOT	A.-Sax. *sceót*, *sceát*, angle or corner (of land), field; sometimes corruption of A.-Sax. *s-holt*, the *s* being the genitive or possessive suffix of the first element of the name; *holt* = wood.
STAN	A.-Sax. *stán*, stone, rock; castle. Bosworth and Toller (*A.-Sax. Dict.*) have collected the following significations of *stán*: i. stone as a material, ii. a stone, iia. a stone for building, iib. a stone, natural or wrought, serving as a mark, iic. an image of stone, iid. a stone to which worship is paid, iie. a stone containing metal, iif. a precious stone, iig. stone (med.), iii. a rock.
STEAD -X-TETH	O. Nor. *stath(r)*, A.-Sax. *stede*, place.
SUT	A.-Sax. *súth*, south.
THING	O. Nor. *thing*, council, parliament.
THORPE TROP	O. Nor. *thorp*, farm, hamlet, village.

GLOSSARY OF PLACE-NAME COMPONENTS

THWAITE	O. Nor. *thveit*, piece of land, clearing.
TON	A.-Sax. *tún*, enclosure, farmstead, manor, village; mod. town. (Also found in Icelandic.)
WAL (prefix)	(1) A.-Sax. *weall*, wall; (2) A.-Sax. *weald*, forest, wood.
WALL (suffix)	O. Nor. *völlr*, field.
WAR	Most commonly prob. A.-Sax. *wer* (O. Nor. *ver* or *vörr*), weir, dam; fishing-place; (?) landing-place.
WICH } WICK }	(1) A.-Sax. *wíc*, habitation, station, creek, bay; (2) O. Nor. *vík*, creek, bay.
WORTH-Y	A.-Sax. *weorthig*, farmstead, estate.

DOMESDAY ENTRIES.

HUNDRED OF WEST DERBY.

Domesday.	Modern.
Achetun	Aughton.
Acrer	Altcar.
Alretune	Allerton.
Bartune	Barton.
Boltelai	Bootle.
Chenulveslei	Knowsley.
Cherchebi	Kirkby.
Chirchedele	Kirkdale.
Cildeuuelle	Childwall.
Crosebi	Crosby.
Daltone	Dalton.
Derbei	(West) Derby.[1]
Einulvesdel	Ainsdale.
Erengermeles	Ravensmeols.
Esmedune	Smithdown (Lane), Liverpool.
Fornebei	Formby.
Herleshala } Heleshale }	Halsall.
Hinne	Ince (Blundell)
Hitune	Huyton.
Hoiland	(Up) Holland.
Holand	(Down) Holland.
Latune	Lathom.
Leiate	Lydiate.

[1] Domesday records that there belonged to the manor of *Derbei* six berewicks, or subordinate manors, which it does not specify. These are presumed to have been Litherpool or Liverpool, Everton, Thingwall, Garston, part of Wavertree, and Great Crosby.

Domesday.	Modern.
Liderlant / Literland	Litherland.
Magele	Maghull.
Mele	(North) Meols.
Melinge	Melling.
Mersha	Mersey.
Neweton	Newton.
Otegrimele / Otringemele	Orrell.
Rabil	Roby.
Sextone	Sefton.
Schelmeresdele	Skelmersdale.
Spec	Speke.
Stochestede	Toxteth.
Torboc	Tarbock.
Torentun	Thornton.
Ulventune / Uvetone	Woolton.
Waletone	Walton (on-the-Hill).
Walintune	Warrington.
Wavretreu	Wavertree.

HUNDRED OF WIRRAL.

Domesday.	Modern.
Bernestone	Barnston.
Blachehol	Blacon.
Calders	Caldy.
Capeles	Capenhurst.
Chenoterie	Noctorum.
Crostone	Croughton.
Estham	Eastham.
Eswelle	Heswall.
Gaitone	Gayton.
Gravesberie	Greasby.
Haregrave	Hargrave.
Hotone	Hooton.
Landechene	Landican.
Lestone	Leighton.
Levetesham	Ledsham.

Domesday.	Modern.
Melas	Meols.
Molintone	Mollington.
Nesse	Ness, or Nesse.
Nestone	Neston.
Optone	Upton.
Pol	(Over) Pool
Pontone	Poulton (Lancelyn).
Potintone	Puddington.
Prestune	Prenton.
Rabie	Raby.
Salhale	Saughall, Soughall.
Sotowiche	Shotwick.
Stanei	Stanney.
Stortone	Storeton.
Sudtone	Sutton.
Tinguelle	Thingwall.
Torintone	Thornton (Hough).
Turstanctone	Thurstaston.
Walea	Wallasey.

LINGUISTIC ABBREVIATIONS, Etc.

A.-S., A.-Sax.	=	Anglo-Saxon or Old English.
Dan.	=	Modern Danish.
Dan.-Norw.	=	Dano-Norwegian.
Du., Dut.	=	Dutch.
E. Eng.	=	Early English.
Fr.	=	French.
Fris.	=	Frisian.
Gael.	=	Gaelic.
Ger.	=	German, *i.e.*, New High German.
Goth.	=	Gothic.
Gr.	=	Greek.
Ir.	=	Irish.
Lat.	=	Latin.
M.E., Mdle. Eng.	=	Middle English (12th to 15th cent.).
Mod. Eng.	=	Modern English.
Nor. Eng.	=	Northern English.
O. Eng.	=	Old English.
O. Fr.	=	Old French.
O. Fris.	=	Old Frisian.
O. H. Ger.	=	Old High German.
O. Nor.	=	Old Norse or Icelandic.
O. Sax.	=	Old Saxon.
Scand.	=	Scandinavian, *i.e.*, common to the Scandinavian languages.
Scot.	=	Scottish.
Swed.	=	Swedish.
Wel.	=	Welsh.

A.-Sax. and O. Nor. ð, þ = *th*.

LIVERPOOL.

WITH the possible exception of London, the name of no English town has excited so much discussion, and been the cause of so much philological brain-cudgelling, as has that of Liverpool. As early as the latter half of last century, the magazines began to take up the tangled etymological thread which had been but little more than touched in passing by the chroniclers of the 16th and 17th centuries. At a later period the columns of *Notes and Queries* were from time to time, and are still occasionally, opened to expressions of opinion upon this evergreen question of the origin of the first two syllables of 'Liverpool.'

Let us glance at the earliest recorded spellings of the name. The most ancient deed in which it is found belongs to the time of Richard I (1189-1199): the form here is *Leverpol*. In King John's charter, 1207, we have *Liverpul*;[1] in that of Henry III., 1229, *Leverepul*; but in the Testa de Nevill (fol. 371), in a part which bears distinct evidence of having been written in the reign of King John, we find the form *Litherpol*. An analysis which I have made of the spellings of the name of the city in 36 of the earliest (13th cent.) Moore charters and deeds relating to Liverpool[2] gives the following result *Leverpol* 1, *Liverpul* 1, *Liverpol* 2, *Liverpool* 8, while *Lyverpol* occurs no fewer

---

[1] *Liverpul* is also the spelling in the Pipe Roll of 10 John (1209), membrane 10.
[2] The Moore Charters and Documents Relating to Liverpool: Report to the Finance and Estate Committee of the City Council; Part I., by Sir J. A. Picton, 1889. I am indebted for a copy of this first part of the Report (the only part so far printed) to Mr. T. N. Morton, Clerk of the Records, Liverpool.

than 33 times. In the State records of the early part of the succeeding century the spellings are almost uniformly with *v*. Thus in the Close Rolls we have the following forms: 1314, *Lyverpol;* 1323 and 1328, *Liverpol.* In the Open Rolls: 1330, *Liverpool* (as to-day); 1333, *Liverpull* and *Liverpole;* 1337, *Leverpol.* In Rymer's Fœdera: 1323, *Liverpol;* 1327, *Lyverpol;* 1336, *Liverpull.* And the *v* form continued to be by far the more usual until the name definitively settled down into its present spelling; among the most notable exceptions to the *v* rule (apart from the instance already mentioned) being the *Letherpole* of the Ministers' Accounts, Duchy of Lancaster, 1509;[1] the *Litherpole* of the Calendar to Pleadings, Duchy of Lancaster, i. 183 (1547); the *Litherpole* and *Litherpoole* of Camden;[2] the *Litherpoole* of a miscellaneous record of the Duchy of Lancaster, dated 1640-41;[3] and the *Litherpool* of Baxter.[4]

For Camden's "in Saxon Liferpole" there is not the slightest authority, the earliest existing document in which the name occurs belonging, as we have seen, to the end of the 12th century, although there is little doubt that Litherpool or Liverpool was one of the six unspecified berewicks mentioned in Domesday as being attached to the manor of

[1] Selby's Lanc. and Chesh. Records Preserved in the Public Record Office, London (Lanc. and Chesh. Record Soc.), 1882-83, i. 100.

[2] In the first edition of Camden's Britannia (1586, p. 429) the passage relative to Liverpool ran: ". . . ubi Lithepole floret, vulgò Lirpole, à diffusa paludis in modum aqua, ut opinio est, nominatus, qui commodissimus et usitatissimus est in Hyberniam traiectus, elegātia et frequentia, quàm antiquitate celebrior." In the edition of 1607 (p. 612) this paragraph is modified as follows: ". . . ubi Litherpoole patet, Saxonicè Liferpole, vulgò Lirpoole," etc. GIBSON's translation (1772, ii. 146) runs ". . . Liverpool, in Saxon Liferpole, commonly Lirpool; so called (as it is thought) from the water spread there like a fen. It is the most convenient and usual place for setting sail into Ireland, but not so eminent for antiquity as for neatness and populousness." GOUGH translated it (1789, iii. 128): ". . . Litherpoole, Saxon Liferpole, commonly called Lirpoole, from a water extended like a pool, according to the common opinion, where is the most convenient and most frequented passage to Ireland; a town more famous for its beauty and populousness than its antiquity."

[3] Selby's Lanc. and Chesh. Records, etc., i. 33.

[4] Glossarium Antiquitatum Britannicarum, 2nd ed., 1733, p. 213 :— ". . . hodiernum verò loco nomen Lither-pool est, sive *Pigra palus.*" (The present name is really derived from the situation—Litherpool or 'sluggish water').

West Derby (Derbei). Of the other 16th century chroniclers Harrison has :[1] "*Lirepoole*, or as it was called of old, *Liverpoole* haven"; and Leland :[2] "*Lyrpole* alias *Lyverpoole*."

Notwithstanding the much greater frequency of the spelling with *v* compared with that with *th* (the forms without either are, of course, merely slurred renderings of the proper name), it is impossible to say with certainty, from the available historical evidence, whether the original form of the name of the city had *liver* or *lever*,[3] *lither* or *lether*; but the contiguity of Litherland would almost seem to indicate that the spelling with *th* was the primitive one.

In an article in the Supplement to the *Lady's Magazine* for 1774 (p. 676), it is asserted that "the right spelling" of the name of the Mersey port "is 'Leverpool'"; but the article is simply based on Enfield's 'Leverpool,'[4] which was published in that year. Enfield offers no definite etymology of the name; he merely refers (chap. I.) to the hypothetical derivations from the fabulous liver bird, or the seaweed liver, or the Lever family, without manifesting a preference for any one of them. In the *Gentleman's Magazine*, vol. lxxxvii. (1817), pt. ii., p. 508, Mr. W. R. Whatton, of Manchester, traces the etymology to a conjectural A.-Sax. *Liðepul*, which he translates as 'still or quiet lake'; and the elder Baines[5] seemed inclined to agree with his coadjutor hereon. But the A.-Sax. *liðe* is the Mod. Eng. 'lithe,' which would give 'Lithe-pool,' instead of Litherpool.

Enfield's successor, Troughton, experienced not the least difficulty in fixing the etymology of 'Liverpool'—or 'Litherpool,' as he preferred to spell the name. "The word *lither*," he says,[6] "signifies *lower*. *Litherpool* means Lower Pool. Hence the name of the village Litherland, or 'Lower Land'; and of a passage, yet called Litherland Alley, in the neigh-

---

[1] Holinshed's Chronicles, Hooker's ed., 1587, i. 84*b*.
[2] Itinerary, Hearne's 2nd ed., 1744, vii. 44.
[3] The student should not overlook the correspondence entitled "Leverpool or Liverpool?" which was initiated in the Liverpool *Courier* on June 7, 1889, by Mr. Ellis Lever.
[4] An Essay towards the History of Leverpool, based on Mr. George Perry's papers, by William Enfield, 1774.
[5] Hist. of Lancashire, 1836, iiii. 55.
[6] Hist. of Liverpool, 1810, p. 20.

bourhood of Pool Lane." The A.-Sax. word for 'lower,' however, is *neothor*, ' nether.'

The younger Baines worked on somewhat different linguistic lines. He was inclined to think that the *Lider* and *Liter* of Domesday,[1] the *Lever* of the reign of Richard I., the *Lither* of Testa de Nevill, etc., were " all originally the same word, and that they are derived, as has been suggested, from the old Gothic word *lide* or *lithe*, the sea, or from some of the words formed from it : as *lid* and *liter*, 'a ship'; *lithe*, 'a fleet of ships'; *lithesman*, ' a seaman.' "[2] But, as Professor Skeat points out, Gothic has no such word as *liðe* or *lithe*, and it does not mean 'the sea' in Anglo-Saxon. It is an adjective, and signifies 'gentle'—Mod. Eng. *lithe*, 'pliant.' *Lid*, ' a ship,' is from a different root, and has nothing to do with it.

The latest historian of Liverpool, Sir J. A. Picton, found the question altogether too knotty for solution, although he possessed infinitely greater philological knowledge than any of the preceding historians of Liverpool. "The name of Liverpool," he observes, "is even more enigmatical than the seal, and has hitherto baffled all investigators in endeavouring satisfactorily to account for its origin. That the name was originally applied to the water rather than to the land appears to be agreed upon all hands. The embouchure of the small stream was called the Pool down to the time of the formation of the Old Dock."[3] Sir James afterwards pointed out that the notion of giving the name *liver* to a bird (which constitutes the popular etymology) was quite unauthorized, the symbolic Liverpool bird being originally the Eagle of St. John. On this point Dr. Collingwood wrote, over thirty years ago : "In both the ancient and the modern seal [of Liverpool] we have a bird which has neither the long legs of a heron nor the long neck of a liver (?), but is as good a representation of a dove bearing an olive branch as we could expect to see in such a situa-

---

[1] This refers to Litherland, there being (as already stated) no mention of Liverpool in Domesday, except that the *Esmedune* of that Survey is assumed to have been the name of a hamlet situate in or near the present Smithdown Lane, Liverpool.

[2] Hist. of Liverpool, 1852, p. 58.

[3] Memorials of Liverpool, 1875, i. 40.

tion. The etymology of the name of Leverpool, or Liverpool, is doubtless topographical rather than heraldic or armorial."[1]

Now let us note the most recent expert opinion upon the question of the etymology of 'Liverpool.'

In *Notes and Queries*, February 29, 1896, p. 173, Professor Skeat writes: ". . . we see that the name *liver* was certainly applied to some kinds of the iris and the bulrush which grew in pools, whence it appears that liver-pool meant originally neither more nor less than 'a pool in which livers grew,' meaning by *liver* some kind of waterflag or bulrush."

To this Canon Taylor replied (*Notes and Queries*, March 21, 1896, p. 233): "Professor Skeat concludes that the *liver* in Liverpool, Livermere, and Liversedge denotes some kind of iris, waterflag, or bulrush, which grew in pools or meres. An obvious difficulty is that while the mere at Livermere was a freshwater mere in which waterflags or bulrushes might grow, the pool at Liverpool is [Canon Taylor was evidently unaware that the pool is filled up] a saltwater pool, in which no such growths are possible." The Canon adds that the meaning of 'Litherland' would throw light on the signification of 'Litherpool' or 'Liverpool.'

But Professor Skeat had already (March 4) written to me as follows: "I am aware that some documents have *Lither* . . .; but if that is right the name also makes perfect sense as it stands, being the O. Eng. *lither*, an extremely common word, meaning 'bad,' and so 'dirty' or 'disagreeable.' Shakespeare uses it in the sense of 'stagnant' or 'sluggish,' as applied to the air, in a passage explained by me some years ago" (1 Hen. VI. 4, 7, 21). And again (March 9) he wrote: "It [*lither* or any of its dialectic variations] is used all sorts of ways. Thus *lether sti* is 'a bad road.' I see no great difficulty over *lither-pool.*"

We have already observed that Baxter explained *Litherpool* as *Pigra palus*, or 'sluggish water.' *Lither* is, more-

---

[1] The Historical Fauna of Lancashire and Cheshire, *Proceedings* Lit. and Phil. Soc. Liverpool, vol. xviii. (1863-64), p. 170.

over, well known as a Northern dialect-word, meaning 'sluggish,' 'idle,' 'lazy.'[1]

If, however, we were to accept Professor Skeat's theory of a 'dirty pool,' what are we to say of 'Litherland' (Domesday *Liderlant* and *Literland*)? I can scarcely think that it was ever intended to designate this particular district 'bad land.' We must, too, pass by the would-be derivation from a hypothetical Celtic *Llyrpwll* (Welsh *llyr*, 'brink,' 'shore,' 'sea'). The A.-Sax. *púl* (O. Nor. *pollr*), 'pool,' is admittedly from the Cymric *pwll*, as a general thing; but it clearly does not follow that Liverpool is necessarily of Welsh origin. Besides, *pwll* in Welsh bi-elemental place-names, in accordance with the genius of the language, is invariably a prefix, as in 'Pwllheli'; and, furthermore, while (as we have observed) 'Liverpool' or 'Litherpool' can be slurred into *Lirpool*, it is hardly conceivable that *Llyrpwll* could be extended into 'Liverpool' or 'Litherpool.'

It would seem that we must rather look to the Teutonic *hlith*, 'a slope,' to supply the much-sought-for etymology. This word is cognate with Lat. *clivus*, 'a gentle ascent,' which exactly tallies with the physiography of Litherland, and the course of the old Pool. It is, however, somewhat doubtful whether the A.-Sax. *hlith* or the O. Nor. *hlith* was the original etymon. Were we to accept the former, it would be necessary to assume that the *er* constituting the second syllable of 'Litherpool' and 'Litherland' was a phonetic intrusion, owing to the difficult vocal combination presented by *thp*. This is, perhaps, a rather unusual assumption with respect to a place-name; but we are not altogether without historical evidence for such reasoning. Kemble says,[2] referring to the common Anglo-Saxon legal terms, and those relating to customs and usages occurring in charters: "The Normans could not even spell the words, hence they write *griderbryce*, *friderbryce*, for *griðbryce* [breach of covenant], *friðbryce* [breach of peace], their own contraction for *der* bearing a distant resemblance to the Saxon ð

---

[1] *Lither* is glossed 'idle,' 'lazy,' in both the Lancashire Glossary (1875-82) and the Cheshire Glossary (1884-86) of the English Dialect Society, as well as in Sir J. A. Picton's South Lancashire Dialect, *Proceedings* Lit. and Phil. Soc. Liverpool, vol. xix. (1864-65), p. 35.

[2] Codex Diplomaticus, i. xliii.

[*dh* or *th*]."[1] This is exactly what may have happened in the case of Litherland, which in Domesday is spelled *Liderlant* and *Literland*, and later, *Litterland*, owing to the difficulty experienced by the Norman French in the articulation of the *th* or *dh* sound—*th* as in 'thank,' *dh* as in 'then.'

On the other hand, if we accept the Norse *hlíth*, which figures in various Scandinavian place-names, there is no necessity to assume a phonetic intrusion, because the genit. sing. case of the word in that language is *hlíthar*, compared with *hlithes* in Anglo-Saxon. In Old Norse we find *hlíthar-brún*, 'the edge of a slope,' *hlíthar-fótr*, 'the foot of a slope,' so that there would not be much difficulty about *hlíthar-land*, 'the land of the slope' or 'the slope land,' and *hlíthar-pollr*, 'the pool of the slope'—in fact, *Hlítharlönd* (*lönd*, pl. of *land*) occurs in the Icelandic record, the Landnámabók.[2] It is scarcely necessary to point out that the Norse element in the vicinity of Liverpool was very strong; and the appropriation of creeks and sea-pools, and of land adjacent to the coast, was a well-known characteristic of the ancient Norwegians and Danes, as, indeed, the name *Vik*-ing implies. It should be mentioned that this derivation from the Old Norse is that which recommends itself both to the Lecturer in Icelandic in University College, Liverpool (Rev. J. Sephton), and to the Professor of Latin in that institution (Dr. Strong).

It only remains to account for the presumed transition from the *th* to the *v* sound in the case of Liverpool. This is a very simple matter. Max Müller published[3] a diagram showing how easily *th* was changed into *f* or *v*, and quoted a well-known German authority[4] in reference hereto. Dr.

---

[1] As to intrusive *r* see Skeat's Notes on English Etymology, *s.v. listre, Transactions* Philological Soc., 1885-86, pp. 1 *sqq.*; also a paper by Dr. Stock on the Influence of Analogy as Explaining Certain Examples of Unoriginal *l* and *r*; *ibid.* pp. 260 *sqq.*; and compare Nidderdale, *i.e.*, the dale of the River Nidd.

[2] Compare also *Lithar-fylki* (*fylki* = *folk*), mentioned in the 12th cent. Danish History of Saxo Grammaticus, *lib.* v., which place is identified by Holder (Saxonis Grammatici Gesta Danorum, ed. 1886, p. 702) with Lier, near Drammen, in Norway.

[3] Science of Language, 2nd ser., 1864, p. 175.

[4] Arendt, Beiträge zur Vergleichenden Sprachforschung, i. 425.

Morris wrote:[1] "The spirants interchange with one another: $f = th$. Children often say *fumb* for 'thumb.' *Cf.* 'dwarf,' Mdle. Eng. *dwerth* and *dwerg* = O. Eng. *thweorh*; Russian Fedor = Theodore." With the uneducated Londoners, too, $th = f$ or v ('with' is pronounced *wiv*), and this is attributable to Norman-French influence. We have also such instances as that supplied in 'The Carved Stones of Islay,' where Mr. R. C. Graham refers to a slab with the inscription, "John Heves, marchand in lever [leather], 1702." The cognate form in Latin (*clivus*) of Teutonic *hlith* has already been noted.

The reason why 'Litherland' did not suffer the mutation with 'Litherpool' is, I think, sufficiently obvious. Litherland, until comparatively recent times, has been a remote and secluded village. Liverpool, as a seaport, after King John developed an interest in it, became more and more subject to extraneous and distracting influences. On the same principle the Icelanders have, by their isolation, preserved the language of their Norse ancestors almost intact, while their brethren, the inhabitants of easily-accessible Scandinavia, have broken it up into modern Norwegian, Danish, and Swedish.

[1] Historical English Grammar, 1875, p. 44.

THE PLACE-NAMES OF THE LIVERPOOL DISTRICT.

I.—HUNDRED OF WEST DERBY.

Abram.—This name affords a curious instance of what some philologists term 'folk assimilation.' The ancient designation was *Edburgham* or *Adburgham*.[1] The place was therefore originally the *hám* or home of a Saxon proprietress named Eadburh (*burh* being a termination of feminine names only).

Aigburth.—The name of the headquarters of the Liverpool Cricket Club represents 'the place of the oaks '— A.-Sax. *ác*, 'oak,' combined with a derivative of *beran*, 'to bear,' 'to produce.' In the Ministers' Accounts of Whalley Monastery, 28-29 Henry VIII. (1537-1538), Lanc. and Chesh. Rec'd Soc., vol. vii., 1882, we have the spelling *Ackeberth*.

Ainsdale.—The Domesday *Einulvesdel*, and the subsequent variations of that name, all imply 'the dale-land (A.-Sax. *del*) belonging to Einulph or Eanulf,' which was a fairly common Saxon name, contracted from Earnwulf, that is, Eagle-Wolf.

Aintree.—The name of this famous racing resort, the Rev. Ed. Powell, of Lydiate—who has devoted much time to the study of old deeds relating to the Ormskirk district—informs me, is nearly always spelled Aintree

[1] Chancery Rolls, 7 Henry IV. (1406), membrane 6; Lanc. and Chesh Rec'd Soc., vol. viii., 1883.

or Ayntree[1] in ancient documents; and as to this day there is a conspicuous absence of large plant-life in the district there seems no reason to doubt that Aintree (A.-Sax. án-treów) means simply 'One Tree.' In fact, upon this very point Professor Skeat writes to me: "We have 'Ainsty,' single or one path (narrow path for one); and I know a 'One-Tree Hill' myself."

Allerton.—This is a common English place-name, meaning 'the alder enclosure or farmstead'—A.-Sax. *alr*, 'alder,' combined with the usual *tún*. The Allerton of the West Derby Hundred occurs in Domesday as *Alretune*.

Alt.—The name of this stream has a certain Teutonic appearance, *alt* being modern German for 'old'—A.-Sax. *eald*.[2] Alt is the name of a river in Central Europe, and it has an alternative appellation, Aluta, which might recall the A.-Sax. *alútan*, 'to bend,' or *aleát*, 'bent down,' with reference to the peculiar and decided way in which the Lancashire Alt bends downwards or southwards where it approaches its embouchure. But there can be no doubt that, as in the case of so many river-names in England, 'Alt' must be referred, like 'Douglas' (black water), the name of a neighbouring river, and 'Gowy' (Welsh *gwy*, or *wy*, 'water'), a river at the southern end of the Wirral peninsula, as well as 'Dee,' to Celtic sources—in this instance to the Gael. *alt*, 'a stream' (*altán*, 'a streamlet'), a name which, naturally generally combined with an adjective-suffix, occurs frequently in Gaelic-speaking districts.

Altcar, near Formby, is enclosed on three sides by the waters of the Alt and its affluents; and *car* is a common word in this part of Lancashire for 'moss-land'—Mdle. Eng. *car* or *ker*, O. Nor. *kiarr*, Swed. *kärr*, 'marshy ground.' Baines ('Lanc.,' 1870, ii. 405) says: "Altcar seems to be the Domesday *Acrer*, half a carucate of waste land held by Uctred; but no other mention is made of this place until 21 Edward I. (1293), when an action was tried between the King and the Abbot of Mira Vallis, or Merivale, as to the right of the latter to one carucate of land in *Altekar* . . .

---

[1] *Ayntre* occurs in the Nonarum Inquisitiones (*temp*. Edw. III.) fol. 40ᵇ.
[2] The Scandinavian languages differ from the Germanic in retaining a different root for 'old'—O. Nor. *gamall*.

As appears from several maps, a hamlet called Altmouth formerly existed at the mouth of the River Alt; and it is supposed to have been overwhelmed by inroads of sand, similar to those which drove the inhabitants of Formby to remove their church and village inland. The remains of houses have been found buried in the sand immediately contiguous to the railway station, Hightown, which is on the site assigned to Altmouth in the township of Ince."

Anfield.—A part of Everton, originally Hangfield, or Hanging-fields, in allusion to the deeply sloping or hanging nature of the ground. Syers says:[1] "In the 3rd Henry VII. anno 1488, an inquisition was taken at Walton, which shows that the boundary of the south part of Walton, 'beginning at Carton Cross, and following to Darling Dale, and to the east end thereof, and so over the Breck, by an ancient ditch on the lands of Everton, called *Hangfield*, on the south part of the common of pasture of Walton,'" etc. He adds: "All the lands of Everton were known by the names of Hangfield, Whitefield, and Netherfield"; and he then appends a footnote: "This word [Hangfield] is frequently written 'Hongfield,' and by some writers 'Honghfield.' I prefer *Hangfield*, that name being derived from 'hanging, or sloping field.' To strengthen the propriety of my orthography in this particular instance, it may be as well to state that in Gore's paper of 26th July, 1810, certain fields of Walton are advertised as follows: 'Fields in Walton-on-the-Hill, called Hanging-fields.'"

Arbury.—The Testa de Nevill has *Herbury* (fol. 396) and *Herebur*' (fol. 398^b), which is exactly how a Norman scribe would write down the spoken 'Arbury'; so we must consider the *h* in the Testa to be intrusive or unoriginal. It is difficult, without evidence of Saxon spelling, to give the meaning of *Ar* with anything approaching certainty. I do not favour A.-Sax. *ǽrra*, 'old,' but rather think that Arbury was perhaps originally a simple earth-fortification—A.-Sax. *eorth-burh* (*cf.* A.-Sax. *heorth* = Mod. Eng. 'hearth'); and this derivation would seem to be confirmed by the form *Erdbury*, which is found in a Duchy of Lancaster document of 18 Henry VII. (1502-3).

[1] Hist. of Everton, 1830, p. 19.

Atherton.—This place occurs in the Testa de Nevill (fols. 396, 398ᵇ, and 408) as *Aderton*. *d* and *ð* (th), it is well known, were constantly interchangeable in Early English: the word 'gather' is from the A.-Sax. *gaderian*, while 'murder' is from A.-Sax. *morthor*. A small stream, which at one point expands into a pool, runs through the township, and there seems no reason to doubt that Atherton is an equivalent of Broughton or Brocton, the *tún* or farmstead by the brook, and is derived, as to its first element, from the A.-Sax. *ǽdre* (compare Swed. *åder*), 'fountain,' 'watercourse.' It is true that Bosworth ('A.-Sax. Dict.,' 1838), on the authority of Lye ('Dict. Sax., etc.,' Manning's ed., 1772), gave *æther* as meaning 'a field,' which would make Atherton a synonym of Felton, the *tún* on an open field or plain; but Lye took *æther* from Ælfric's 'Colloquy,' where it is glossed *ager* (field), while later vocabularists declare *æther*, as it there occurs, to be a mistake for *æcer*, 'field.' Thus Wülcker, editing Wright,[1] prints *æcer* in the 'Colloquy,' and adds a note: "The MS. reads distinctly *æther*, which is no doubt an error for *æcer*."

Aughton.—Aughton, or *Aghton*, as the name was spelled in the reign of Edward II. (1307-1327), might at first sight appear to be referable to the Gael. *auch* and the Ir. *agh*, *augh* (*achadh*), 'field'; but seeing that the spelling *Acton* occurs in the times of John and Henry III. (1199-1272), and bearing in mind that the *ch* in the Domesday *Achetun* (as our Aughton figures in the Norman Survey) generally represents hard *c* (k), it seems but reasonable to assume that Aughton was simply 'the oak farmstead,'[2] A.-Sax. *ác*, 'oak'—just as the Aughton in Yorkshire was.

Bamfurlong, the name of a village near Wigan, is literally 'the tree furrow-length'—A.-Sax. *beám* (Ger. *baum*), 'tree'; *furh*, 'furrow'; *lang*, 'long.' A furlang, or furlong, appears to have originally been a square as well as a long measure, "having," says Kemble,[3] "determinate length and width, and forming a fixed portion of an acre."

---

[1] Anglo-Saxon and Old English Vocabularies, 2nd ed., 1884, p. 90.

[2] It should, however, be mentioned that the spelling *Asshton* occurs in the Survey of 1320-1346, Chetham Soc., vol. lxxiv., 1868. The ash was the favourite tree of the Anglo-Saxons.

[3] Codex Diplomaticus, iii. xxv. But see footnote p. 45.

Bankhall.—Bank Hall, close to the *bank* of the Mersey, was long the residence of the ancient Liverpool family of More or Moore. No trace of the mansion now remains.

Barton.—Domesday spelling *Bartune.* Barton is a very common English place-name, derived from the A.-Sax. *bere-tún,* ' barley yard,' ' grange.' It is distinct from BURTON, which see in the Wirral Section.

Bedford.—The name of this township does not occur in the earliest extant records; it is not mentioned in Domesday or the Testa de Nevill. It seems, however, to have formerly been spelt *Bedeford;* and the original appellation may have been identical with that of the like-named Midland county town, which meant 'the ford of Bedica,' the sequence in Anglo-Saxon deeds relating to this important place being briefly: *Bedicanford* (*Bedican,* genit. sing. of the personal name Bedica), *Bedanford, Bedeford.* Or the Lancashire Bedford may originally have simply been *Bedanford,* ' the ford of Beda.'

Bickerstaffe.—The earliest recorded spelling of this name, *Bikerstat,* seems to be in the Testa de Nevill (fol. 402^b). In ancient Burscough MSS. *Bykyrstath* repeatedly occurs, and even as late as 1517 we find *Bekerstath,* although the termination *staff* or *staffe* had apparently been used before that date. The first portion of the name is probably from a personal appellation, while the last syllable must be attributable to the O. Nor. *stathr* (A.-Sax. *stede*) ' a place.' As a personal name Biker or Bicker may be from two sources. The O. Nor. *bikarr,* ' a large drinking cup,' is still with us in the Scot. *bicker* and the Eng. *beaker;* and Jamieson[1] says that *bikarr* " was the term used to denote the cup drunk by the ancient Scandinavians in honour of their deceased heroes." But more likely the origin of the personal appellation is to be found in the O. Nor. *byggia* (Dan. *bygge,* Swed. *bygga*), ' to build,' whence the Scot. and Nor. Eng. *big* or *byg,* ' to build,' and *biggar,* ' builder.'

[1] Scottish Dictionary, under *bicker,* quoting Keysler, Antiq. Septent., pp. 352-354.

Billinge.—This was a settlement of the Saxon Billing family,[1] and, according to the canon now accepted, an original, or parent, or ancestral settlement, as distinct from the offshoot which would be implied by a Billington or a Billingham.

Birkdale.—On the face of it this name would simply represent 'the dale of the birches'—O. Nor. *björk*, 'birch,' and Scand. *dal;* but as the earliest found spelling is *Breck-en-le-Dale*, which occurs in a deed of 6 Edward I. (1278)—Duchy Records—by which Sir Robt. Blundell, son of Adam, lord of Aynosdale (Ainsdale), released certain lands to his son, birches have apparently nothing to do with the etymology of Birkdale. The exact meaning of the dialect-word 'breck' is somewhat doubtful; it seems to vary in different parts of the Anglian country to which it is confined. Thus the 'Hist. Eng. Dict.' notes from local authorities that in Norfolk and Suffolk 'breck' signifies a large field, while in Northumberland, etc., it represents 'a portion of a field cultivated by itself.' Some believe that a breck was, in all Teutonic countries, originally a piece of land that was either temporarily or permanently idle or waste in the midst of a cultivated tract. The Mod. Eng. equivalent appears to be 'brake' or 'bracken,' which are connected with the Dan.-Norw. *bregne*, 'brake,' 'fern'; Dan.-Norw. *brak*, 'fallow'; Swed. *bräken*, 'brake,' 'fern'; Ger. *brach*, 'fallow,' etc. We should not, however, overlook the Norse word *brekka*, 'a slope,' which is frequently found in Icelandic local names and will doubtless account for some English 'Brecks.'

Blundellsands.—This place, topographically, is practically identical with Crosby, where is the residence of the Blundell family. "Within the last forty years," say Baines's editors,[2] "Great Crosby has very considerably increased, having become a regular place of residence for Liverpool merchants; and the present proprietor of Little Crosby has appropriated a long track of sandhills on the coast for building purposes, under the name of *Blundell-Sands*."

---

[1] Birch's ed. (1876) of Kemble's Saxons in England, i. 458.
[2] Lanc., 1870, ii. 398.

Bold, Bootle.—The names of these places present no etymological difficulty. The A.-Sax. *bold, bolt, botl*, meant 'house,' 'dwelling,' 'village.' In Domesday the name of the place which is now called Bootle was spelled *Boltelai*. Upon this point Prof. Skeat writes to me: "I suppose that, in *Boltelai*, the *boltel* alone represents 'Bootle,' and the *ai* is a suffix." In the Testa de Nevill, fol. 403 (for Bootle), we have the spelling *Botle;* in a document dated 1541 *Botill* occurs. Leo's identification of A.-Sax. *botl* and *bold* with Ger. *büttel*[1] is now shown not to be correct.

Bryn.—This Lancashire place-name has no connection with the Wel. *bryn*, 'hill.' It is probably of Norman-French origin, as Alan le Brun (O. Fr. *brun*, 'brown'), who is mentioned in the Testa de Nevill (fol. 403) as holding by ancient tenure two bovates of land for 6s. of Henry de Lee, Sheriff of Lancashire in 1274 and 1282, is reputed to have given his name to Brun or Bryn Hall. The ultimate source of Fr. *brun* is, however, the O. H. Ger. *brún*, so that the origin is Teutonic. See Stappers's 'Dict. Synopt. d'Étymologie Française,' 1894, p. 506, and compare A.-Sax. *brún*, Ger. *braun*, 'brown.'

Burscough.—The spelling in 1285 was *Burschow;* in the Survey of 1320-1346, Chetham Soc., vol. lxxiv., 1868, we have *Burschoge*. The latter element in the name is allied to the Mdle. Eng. *shawe*, A.-Sax. *sceaga*, 'thicket,' 'small wood,' and is from the O. Nor. *skógr* (Dan. *skov*, Swed. *skog*). The first element may be from a personal name, or it is perhaps connected with Mod. Eng. 'bur' or 'burr'; *cf.* Dan. *borre*, 'burr,' 'burdock.' Or the grove may have contained a *búr*, or bower.

Burtonwood. — Burton = A.-Sax. *búr-tún*, 'the boor farm'; compare Chorlton. But see the Wirral BURTON.

Childwall.—The Domesday spelling is *Cildeuuelle*, which shows that the name of this township was pronounced at the end of the eleventh century practically as it is to-day; in 1259 *Childwalle* occurs; in the Testa de Nevill we have *Childewale* and *Childewall*. Other renderings are *Chelde-*

[1] Die Angelsächsischen Ortsnamen (Rectitudines Singularum Personarum), Halle, 1842, p. 36.

well, *Chidewell, Chidwall* (1624), *Chilwell* (1760), and even *Kydewell*. The second syllable is homonymous with the *-wall* of 'Thingwall'—O. Nor. *völlr* (dat. sing. *velli*), 'field'; and we have the O. Nor. *kelda* (Dan. *kilde*, Swed. *källa*, Nor. Eng. *keld*), 'well,' 'spring.' The Mod. Eng. equivalent of Childwall is therefore 'Wellfield' or 'Springfield.'

Chowbent derives its name from a bent (A.-Sax. *beonet*), or common, which was owned by one Chew or Chow.[1]

Croft.—A.-Sax., 'a small farm.'

Cronton.—The name of this place occurs in the Testa de Nevill as *Grohinton* (fol. 396^b), and as *Crohinton* (fol. 398^b)[2]; but in 1562 we find a spelling—*Crawenton*—which (unless we have here the inevitable personal appellation) would imply that the original Saxon *tún*, or farmstead, received its designation from a settlement of crows—A.-Sax. *cráwe* (pl. *cráwan*), 'a crow.'[3]

Crosby.—The name of this Norse settlement was spelled *Crosebi* in Domesday, *Crossby* in the Testa de Nevill; and by 1645 it had reached its present stage (Crosby). This was 'the hamlet of the (stone) cross'—O. Nor. *kross*, combined with O. Nor. *býr*, Scand. *by*, 'village,' 'town.' It is recorded in Baines ('Lanc.,' 1870, ii. 396) that "An ancient cross stands in Little Crosby. This was formerly the object of a pleasing village festival called 'The Flowering of the Cross.' Mr. Nicholas Blundell, in an unpublished diary of the first quarter of last century, makes annual mention of it, as having attended it with his family."

Crossens.—The earliest forms of the name, viz.,

---

[1] Unpublished MS. Notes of Dorning Rasbotham, written 1787; Baines, Lanc., 1870, ii. 202.

[2] This difference in the initial letter is not here of much significance: the Romans at one time did not distinguish between the sound of C (k) and G hard; but eventually the necessity of discrimination became evident, and G was formed by slightly modifying C. See the author's essay, 'A Fascinating Science,' in the *Educational Times*, January, 1896, p. 35; and, for the vagaries of G in another tongue, his paper, 'The Humours of a Great Language—Russian,' in the *Journal of Education*, December, 1894, p. 710.

[3] *Cráwe* forms one of the select body of onomatopoetic or imitative words.

Crossnes in the Scarisbrick deeds (thirteenth century), and *Crosnes* in the Nonarum Inquisitiones, fol. 40^b (*temp.* Edw. III.), point to but one etymology—O. Nor. *kross*, 'cross,' and *nes*, 'a ness or slip of land,' in allusion to the comparatively elevated position occupied by the place under discussion between Martin Mere and the estuary of the Ribble. The Rev. W. T. Bulpit says that Archdeacon Clarke used to argue that Crossens meant Cross Sands! The ancient cross of the township has been succeeded by a maypole.

Croxteth.—In 1228 we find the spelling *Croxstath*. The latter element may be referred to the O. Nor. *stathr* (A.-Sax. *stede*, Ger. *stadt*), 'a stead,' 'a place'; while the first syllable is probably the O. Nor. *krókr* (Dan. *krog*, Swed. *krok*), which signified (1) anything crooked, (2) a nook or corner, (3) a personal name,[1] as in the place-name Króksfjörthr, which would make, in Mod. Eng., Croxforth.

Cuerdley.—In the Survey of 1320-1346, Chetham Soc., vol. lxxiv., 1868, we find *Cuerdesleghe* mentioned as one of the members of the manor of 'Wydnesse.' The first element is no doubt a personal name, the second being from the common A.-Sax. *leáh* (ley, lea), 'pasture-land.'

Culcheth.—After careful study of the evidence which is so far available, I am unable to agree with the conclusion come to by many, both locally and extraneously, that this place is the *Cealchýth* or *Cælchýth* which is so frequently mentioned in Saxon charters, and was upon various occasions the scene of *gemóts*, or meetings of the Supreme Council of the Anglo-Saxons, as well as of synods of their Church. It is true, as Mr. Robson, a local antiquary of considerable repute, pointed out,[2] that one of the farm-houses is, or was, moated round and called the 'Old Abbey'; but I do not see how we can get behind the cold fact that A.-Sax. *Cealc-hýth* means 'the chalk hithe, wharf, or landing-place,' and that there is no chalk at Culcheth, nor any river. Besides, Bosworth[3] and Thorpe,[4] as well as Toller,[5] unite

---

[1] Krok the Peasant (Croc Agrestis)—Saxonis Grammatici Gesta Danorum, *lib.* viii., Holder's ed., 1886.
[2] Baines, Lanc., 1870, ii. 218.   [3] A.-Sax. Dict., 1838.
[4] A.-Sax. Chronicle, 1861.
[5] A.-Sax. Dict. (Bosworth and Toller), almost completed.

in assigning (though Thorpe doubtfully) Cealchýth to Challock, or Chalk, in Kent. In early post-Conquest times Culcheth was styled *Culchet, Kulchet,* and *Culchit.* The natives of the place carry apocope still further, and, we are told, pronounce the name *Kilsha.* As to the etymology of the name, if we discard the idea of the common Celtic prefix *kil, i.e. cill* (church) from Lat. *cella,* 'cell,' and of the Gael. *coill,* 'wood,' which usually gives the prefix *cul* or *kil* in Anglicized names,[1] we may note that *Cul* is an Anglo-Saxon patronymic,[2] as embodied in Culingworth or Cullingworth, while the second syllable of the name might be referable to the A.-Sax. *cete* (chete), 'cottage,' 'cell.' The form *Cultheth,* occurring in the Nonarum Inquisitiones (*temp.* Edw. III.), fol. 40[b], suggests, however, a possible original A.-Sax. *Ceald-hǽth,* 'Cold Heath.'

Cunscough.—This name occurs in the Survey of 1320-1346, Chetham Soc., vol. lxxiv., 1868, as *Conescoughe.* The meaning is 'rabbit grove'—Mdle. Eng. *coning, cuning, cunny,* etc. (Scand. *kanin*), through O. Fr. ultimately from Lat. *cuniculus,* 'cony,' 'rabbit'; and the dialectic survival of O. Nor. *skógr* (Swed. *skog,* Dan.-Norw. *skov*), 'grove,' 'wood.' See HARGRAVE in the Wirral section. The cony or rabbit does not appear to have been introduced into England until after the advent of the Normans.

Dallum.—'In the dales'—dative plural of A.-Sax. *dæl,* 'dale.'

Dalton, near Skelmersdale, is referred to in Domesday as *Daltone*—"the farmstead in the dale"—A.-Sax. *dæl-tún.*

Ditton.—The name was formerly spelled *Dytton.* The English Dittons are generally traceable to A.-Sax. *Dictún,* 'a diked or ditched enclosure'—A.-Sax. *dic,* masc. = 'dike,' fem. = 'ditch.' 'Dike' and 'ditch' are therefore doublets. In excavating a ditch a dike was necessarily thrown up. The name Ditton is consequently somewhat analogous to Walton where the latter refers to a wall or rampart and not to a weald, wold, or wood.

Douglas.—The name of the river which flows through Wigan, and upon the banks of which, in contiguity to that

---

[1] Sir H. Maxwell, Scottish Land Names, 1894, p. 105.
[2] Birch's ed. of Kemble's Saxons in England, 1876, i. 450.

town, tradition avers that King Arthur achieved several victories over the Saxons,[1] is derived from the Gael. *dubh* (doo), 'black,' and *glaise, glas,* 'water.' "This syllable *glas*," says Sir Herbert Maxwell,[2] "has two meanings; as an adjective it means 'green' or 'grey' [Wel. *glas*, 'blue,' 'grey,' 'green'] probably cognate with the Lat. *glaucus;* as a substantive it means 'a stream.' Thus Dunglas is Gael. *dùn glas,* 'green hill'; but Douglas is *dubh glas*, 'the dark stream.'" Some have argued that 'Douglas' means 'dark green,' 'water' or 'river' being understood; but Joyce, in both his works on Irish topographic nomenclature,[3] gives 'Douglas' as representing 'dark or black stream,' as above.

Downholland, near Altcar, occurs in Domesday as *Holand*, which is probably a corruption of the A.-Sax. *holtland,* 'wood-land' (Ger. *Holz,* 'wood'); *t* between two *l*'s would soon drop. There is a Holt Lane not very far from the township, which latter acquired the later prefix 'Down' in order to distinguish it from Upholland (near Wigan), which lies high and contiguous to moors and woods. It was at one time thought that the name of the Dutch kingdom meant 'the low or hollow land' (Dut. *hol,* A.-Sax. *hol,* Ger. *hohl,* 'hollow'); but a ninth century document was discovered in which the spelling *Holtland* occurred, and 'woodland' was as naturally applicable to the country as 'low land.'

Eccleston.—A fairly common Lancashire ecclesiastical place-name, the equivalent of 'Churchtown'—'Eccles' coming through Late Latin, like Fr. *église,* Wel. *eglwys,*

---

[1] The fourteenth-century Monk of St. Werburgh's, Chester, Ranulf Higden, referring to Arthur's battles with the Saxons, says (Polychronicon, *lib.* v.) there were four "super flumen Duglas ... Hodie fluvius ille vocatur Anglice Duggles, et currit sub urbe de Wygan, per decem miliaria a fluvio de Merscie distante in comitatu Lancastriæ." Trevisa translated this (in 1387) ". . . uppon the ryver Douglas. . . . Now that ryver hatte [is called] Dugglys in Englische, and that ryver renneth under the citee of Wygan, that is ten myle from the ryver Mersea in Lancastreschire."—Polychronicon Ranulphi Higden Monachi Cestrensis, with Trevisa's and another translation, Babbington and Lumby's ed., vol. v. (1874), pp. 328, 329.

[2] Scottish Land Names, 1894, p. 15.

[3] Irish Local Names Explained, 1884, p. 40; Irish Names of Places, 2nd ser., 1875, p. 266.

etc., from Gr. ἐκκλησία, 'an assembly of citizens,' 'the church.'

Everton.—The earliest recorded mention of Everton seems to be in a document of 9 Hen. III. (1225),[1] in which the name is spelled exactly as it is to-day. Everton was, however, probably one of the six unspecified berewicks noted in Domesday as pertaining to the manor of Derbei (West Derby). The late Sir J. A. Picton[2] followed Syers[3] in stating that Everton occurs in Domesday as *Hiretun*. But the context of the passage in Domesday shows that Everton cannot be intended, and that Beamont[4] is probably right in assigning *Hiretun* to Tarleton. There would not at first sight appear to be a connection between the names of Everton and York, yet there is a fairly intimate one. The Saxons transformed the Celto-Roman *Eboracum* or *Everacum* into *Eofor-wic* or *Efer-wic*[5] (the variations in spelling are numerous, but the pronunciation remains practically the same), of which 'York' is a corruption, the *wic* or *wich* (Lat. *vicus*, Gr. οἶκος) being an Anglo-Saxon equivalent of 'habitation,' 'village,' etc. *Eofor* or *efer* means 'a wild boar.' Everton was therefore originally the enclosure or farmstead of Efer or Eofor, which was a tolerably common Saxon name. It occurs, for instance, several times as a personal name in 'Beowulf,' "the oldest heroic poem in any Germanic tongue"; and, compounded, more than once in the famous list of benefactors to the Church of Durham, dating from the ninth century.[6]

Farnworth.—'The fern-farm.' A.-Sax. *fearn* (Ger. *Farn*), 'fern' or 'brake'; A.-Sax. *weorthig*, 'farm,' 'estate.'

Fazakerley, we read, "was long the residence of an ancient family of that name," who, no doubt, derived their cognomen from the place. The origin of the first portion of the name seems obscure, but we can divide the word into

---
[1] Rotuli Litterarum Clausarum, ii. 64b.
[2] Memorials of Liverpool, 1875, ii. 334.
[3] Hist. of Everton, 1830, p. 41.
[4] Domesday Cheshire and Lancashire, 1882, xvb.
[5] Anglo-Saxon ƒ had the sound of *v* wherever possible.
[6] Liber Vitae Ecclesiae Dunelmensis, Stevenson's ed., Surtees Soc. vol. xiii., 1841. Also included in Sweet's Oldest English Texts, Early Eng. Text Soc., 1885, pp. 153 *sqq*.

three Anglo-Saxon vocables: *fas*, 'fringe'; *aker* (*æcer*), '(cultivated) field,' and *ley* (*leáh*), 'meadow,' which might imply 'the meadowland with a certain or particular border or boundary field.' There is no other Fazakerley in England. The nearest approach to it is Fazeley, a place situate upon the border of the counties of Stafford and Warwick. We must reject the idea of a connection with the Gael. *fásach*, which, as an adjective, signifies 'desolate,' 'desert'; as a substantive, (1) 'grassy headland of a ploughed field,' (2) 'wilderness'; but it should be noted that *faws* is a Northern dialect-word for 'fox,'[1] which has entered largely into personal and local nomenclature; and, on the whole, it seems probable that this word forms the first element of 'Fazakerley.' 'A(c)kerley' by itself is an English local and personal name, and it probably had the same signification as 'Acre Dale,' which the 'Hist. Eng. Dict.,' quoting from Halliwell, defines as 'lands in a common field in which different proprietors held portions of greater or less quantities.'[2] I do not attach importance to an isolated case of 'a(c)ker' being found in Cheshire to represent a sheet of water.[3]

Fearnhead.—'The high ground overgrown with ferns'—A.-Sax. *fearn*, 'fern'; *heáfod*, 'head,' 'high ground.'

Formby.—The name of this Scandinavian settlement is given as *Fornebei* in Domesday, and *Forneby* was the spelling in the thirteenth century. The mutation to 'Formby' is simple, the later *m* resulting, phonetically, from the flat

[1] Halliwell, Dict. of Archaic and Provincial Words, 1850.
[2] Much has of late years been written upon the mediæval acre, and authors have differed. It may, however, be said roughly that the open or common field (A.-S. *feld*) was formerly divided into smaller fields, or shots (A.-S. *sceát*), or furlongs (A.-S. *furh-lang*, *i.e.*, furrow-length); these, again, being split up into acres (A.-S. *æcer*) of varying shapes and sizes, but perhaps most usually consisting of four or five selions (Lat. *selio*, Fr. *sillon*), or strips, or beds, separated from each other by balks (A.-S. *balc*), or ridges (A.-S. *hrycg*), or riggs (O. Nor. *hryg(r)*), or linches (A.-S. *hlinc*), or as they were, and are, often styled in the North, rains (O. Nor. *rein*, Ger. *rain*), *i.e.*, unploughed strips. See Maitland, Domesday Book and Beyond, 1897, pp. 373 *sqq.*; Gomme, Village Community, 1890, pp. 193, 194; Seebohm, English Village Community, 1884, pp. 2, 106, 384, etc.
[3] Kendrick, Roman Remains Discovered at Wilderspool near Warrington, *Transactions* Chester Archæological Soc., vol. iii., 1885, p. 195.

labial *b* immediately following the liquid *n*. In the same way *Brunburgh* became Bromborough, *Dunbreatan*, Dumbarton. 'Formby' is thought locally to mean 'the pious or holy place.' It is true that the O. Nor. *fórn* (long *o*) represents 'an offering to God'; but I rather think that we must look for an explanation of the first element of the placename to the O. Nor. *forn* (short *o*), 'old' (A.-Sax. *fyrn*). Formby is the most prominent point on the South Lancashire coast, and would probably be the earliest settlement of the Northmen in that district; and when other Norse posts were established this original one might easily be looked upon as 'the old village,' or *Forn-by*.[1] Saxon equivalents are Aldbrough, Oldham, etc. There is only one Formby in Great Britain.

Unfortunately, Old Norse documents do not help us very much in regard to fixing the etymology of the less important Scandinavian settlements in England, especially those on the West Coast. Thus no Lancashire or Cheshire placename is to be traced in the 'Icelandic Sagas, etc., relating to the British Isles,' published by the Rolls Office (text by Vigfusson, 1887; translation by Dasent, 1894), although we meet with *Gríms-bær* (Grimsby), *Hjarta-pollr* (Hartlepool), *Hvíta-býr* (Whitby), *Jór-vík* (York), *Skardha-borg* (Scarborough), *Járna-mótha* (Yarmouth), *Mön* (Man), *Önguls-ey* (Anglesey), etc., in them; and this applies, with stronger reason, to Vigfusson and Powell's 'Corpus Poeticum Boreale,' 1883, and the Danish History of Saxo Grammaticus ('Saxonis Grammatici Gesta Danorum,' Holder's ed., 1886), the first nine books of which History have been translated and edited by Elton and Powell respectively (1894).

Freshfield is 'the field of the fresh-water spring or streamlet,' *fresh* being an old dialect-word for a current of fresh water running into tidal water.[2]

Garston.—This name is referable to the A.-Sax. *gærs*,

[1] Compare *forne*, 'first,' 'former,' 'fore,' in Halliwell's Dict. of Archaic and Provincial Words, 1850; and *forne*, 'anterior,' in the fifteenth-century vocabulary Promptorium Parvulorum, Way's ed., Camden Soc., 1843-65; also the place-name *Fornhagi* (Oldfield) in the celebrated Icelandic record, the Landnámabók.

[2] "He shall drink nought but brine; for I'll not show him
Where the quick *freshes* are."—Shak., Tempest, iii. 2.

'grass,' combined with the usual *tún*. It denotes the use which the early Saxon proprietor made of the land.

Gateacre.—'The road-field'—Mdle. Eng. *gate*, 'way,' 'road' (compare Scand. *gata* (*gade*), 'way,' 'road,' 'street'; A.-Sax. *geat*), and *acre* (*æcer*), 'field.' I think, all things considered, that this is a more probable etymology than 'goat-field'—A.-Sax. *gát*, 'goat.' The name of Gateshead (-on-Tyne), which was long thought to mean 'Goat's Head,' is now concluded to represent 'Road's Head.' See GAYTON in the Wirral Section.

Glazebrook.—The village is named from the stream, which, like Alt and Douglas, bears a Celtic name—Gael. *glaise*, *glas*, 'streamlet.' The invading Saxons added *bróc* (brook) to the to them meaningless Erse term *glaise*. The form *Glasebroc* occurs in the Nonarum Inquisitiones, *temp.* Edw. III., fol. 40.

Golborne.—The early spellings of the name of this place, namely, *Goldborne* (1301), and *Goldburn* in the Testa de Nevill, perhaps indicated the yellow colour of the burn or brook whence the township derived its appellation.

Haigh.—'The hedged enclosure'—A.-Sax. *haga*.

Hale.—In the thirteenth century we read of the "lands of Hales" and the "town of Halis." The name Hale is fairly common in England, and sometimes refers to a large residence or hall—A.-Sax. *heall*. We thus have an ancient Hale Hall here, and there is a Hale Hall in Cumberland; but both 'hale' and 'hall' are frequently referable to A.-Sax. *heal(h)*—O. Nor. *hall(r)*—'a slope,' pl. *healas* or *halas*; and the early spellings quoted above would seem to lead to the conclusion that the original name of the Lancashire township was intended to signify 'the slopes.'[1]

Halsall.—This place is referred to in Domesday as *Herleshala* and *Heleshale*, while the present spelling Halsall

---

[1] In the Exchequer Lay Subsidy Roll for Lancashire, 1332, edited by Mr. J. Paul Rylands for the *Miscellanies* (vol. ii.) of the Lanc. and Chesh. Rec'd Soc., it is surprising to find that, while only 16 names are returned for Manchester, with a total value of 46 shillings, the now insignificant village of Hale stands with 25 names, and pays the sum of 54 shillings. This Subsidy Roll practically forms a directory of all above the mere peasant class living in Lancashire in 1332.

occurs in 1256. The first element in the name was once foisted by Canon Taylor,[1] following a German fashion, upon the Celtic *hal*, 'salt.' The exact meaning of A.-Sax. *heal(h)*, which is generally rendered *hala* and *hale* in Domesday, has been doubtful to the moderns. Until comparatively recently everybody followed Kemble[2] in his attribution of 'stone house,' 'hall'; but it is now accepted that 'slope' or 'rising ground' is the signification which is often meant, and this assumption is apparently borne out by the Old Norse word *hall(r)*, 'slope,' 'hill.' In many English place-names with the termination under discussion the first element is a personal appellation, as that of the present Halsall doubtless is. There are no grounds for associating the A.-Sax. *sele*, O. Nor. *sal(r)* (dat. and accus. *sal*), 'hall,' 'dwelling,' with Halsall.

Haydock.—It is remarked by Baines or his editors[3] that "this place is supposed to derive its name from the *hedges* of *oak*, or rather the oaks in the hedges, some of which, it is said, were planted as early as the reign of Edward the Confessor"; but this etymology is obviously impossible: it leaves unaccounted for the *d* which is present in all the older renderings of the unique name—*Eydock*, *Haidoc*, *Haydok*, etc. Taken literally the name would mean 'hedge-dock'—A.-Sax. *hege-docce ;* the hedges hereabouts may have been overrun with the troublesome dock or sorrel ; or pasture-land enclosed by a hedge—such enclosure being called in Anglo-Saxon a *haga*—may have been in this condition ; or *Eydock* may be simply the A.-Sax. *eá-docce*, 'water-dock.' In the absence of sufficiently early documental evidence—the place is not mentioned in Domesday or the Testa de Nevill—it is difficult to say with certainty what the modern 'Haydock' originally represented : there do not seem to be any grounds for connecting the name with A.-Sax. *heg*, 'hay.' But, on the whole, the latter element of the name is probably the E. Eng. *doke* or *doak*, 'a hollow'[4]—O. Nor. *dökk*, 'pit,' 'pool ;' the whole name therefore representing 'the hollow place enclosed by a hedge.'

[1] Words and Places, 1864, p. 392.
[2] Codex Diplomaticus, iii. xxix.
[3] Lanc., 1870, ii. 212.
[4] Halliwell, Dict. of Archaic and Provincial Words, 1850.

Hindley.—In the Testa de Nevill (fol. 406) we find *Hindele.* In the Survey of 1320-1346, Chetham Soc., vol. lxxiv., 1868, the name occurs as *Hyndeleghe.* It may have signified 'the hind or hinder meadowland'—A.-Sax. *hindan* and *leáh;* but in view of other similarly-formed local names we must give the preference to an association with the female of the stag.[1] As to 'hind,' a peasant, its Anglo-Saxon etymon *hína,* 'a servant,' invariably appears in place-names as *hin-,* as in the numerous Hintons. There is still another possible, though in this case doubtful, connection: Kemble[2] makes a *hind* or *hynd* represent the third part of the hide, the Anglo-Saxon land-measure of varying acreage.[3]

Hollinfare. — Literally 'the holly ferry' (over the Mersey)—E. Eng. *holin* (A.-Sax. *hole(g)n*), 'holly'; *faru,* 'passage.' The contiguity of Hollin's Green, however, renders it possible that the ferry was attended to by a person named Hollin.

Houghton.—'The farmstead on the heel or projecting ridge of land'—A.-Sax. *hóh,* 'heel,' 'ridge'; *tún,* 'farmstead.'

Hulme.—'Low riparian meadowland'—dialectic variation of A.-Sax. *holm.*

Huyton figured in Domesday as *Hitune.* The name means 'the elevated enclosure or farmstead'—A.-Sax. *heáh* (Mdle. Eng. *hig, hy,* etc.), 'high,' combined with the usual *tún.*

Ince or **Ince Blundell.**—It seems almost natural to fly to the Celtic for the etymology of Ince (Wel. *ynys,* Gael. *innis,* Ir. *inis, ennis,* Scot. *inch,* 'island'); but where Domesday, as in this case, has *Hinne,* and circumstances seem to preclude the theory of an island, or even of low riparian land, it is but reasonable that resort should be had to

---

[1] "The equine species has given to us 'Horsley'; the bovine, 'Cowley,' 'Kinley,' and 'Oxley'; the deer, 'Hartley,' 'Rowley,' 'Buckley' and *Hindley;* the fox, 'Foxley'; the hare, 'Harley'; and the sheep, 'Shipley.'"—Bardsley, English Surnames, 5th ed., 1897, p. 119.

[2] Codex Diplomaticus, iii. xxx.

[3] As Domesday units, Mr. Round (Feudal England, 1895, p. 37) gives 30 acres in the virgate, and 4 virgates in the hide, which therefore represents 120 acres.

another language. In Old Norse we have *inni*, 'inn,' 'abode,' 'house,' 'hall' (there exists an Ince Hall). The genit. sing. of *inni* is *innis*, which would be used with dative significance with the preposition *til*, 'to,' which the genius of the Icelandic language requires should take the genitive case, as in the phrase *ok til sama innis*, 'and to the same house.' *Ines* was the spelling in the reign of Edward III. (1327-1377). Blundell is the patronymic of the owners of the manor.

Kenyon.—In the Testa de Nevill (fol. 405ᵇ) we find mention of Robert le Kenien, from whom this township derives its name. In the Survey of 1320-1346, Chetham Soc., vol. lxxiv., 1868, we have the spelling *Kenean*. It is not quite clear what 'Kenien' or 'Kenean' means. It may be a mutated form of the O. Fr. *chanoine*, 'a canon'; or possibly of O. Fr. *kienin* (*chienin*), 'doglike,' 'canine,' or O. Fr. *kenon*, 'little dog'; compare such names as William le Chien, Eborard le Ken, Thomas le Chene (O. Fr. *chen* (*ken*), 'dog'), quoted from mediæval rolls, as nicknames from the animal kingdom, by Bardsley in his 'English Surnames,' 5th ed., 1897, pp. 492, 534, 567.

Kirkby.—The Domesday *Cherchebi* is the Norse equivalent of the modern English Churchtown—O. Nor. *kirkja* (Dan.-Norw. *kirke*, Swed. *kyrka*), 'church'; O. Nor. *býr* (Scand. *by*), 'settlement,' 'village.'

Kirkdale, the Domesday *Chirchedele*, is the low ground upon which stood the Northmen's church—O. Nor. *kirkja* (Dan.-Norw. *kirke*, Swed. *kyrka*), 'church'; O. Nor. *dalr* (Scand. *dal*), 'dale.'

Knowsley is a corruption of 'Kenulf's Ley'—A.-Sax. *leáh*, 'meadowland'—as the Domesday spelling *Chenulveslei* shows. Kenulf—A.-Sax. *Céne Wulf*, 'Bold Wolf.'

Lathom.—This township and ancient chapelry was noted for many centuries as the seat of the Stanleys. The Domesday spelling of the name was *Latune*. In 1221 we find *Ladhun ;* and not very long afterwards (*temp.* Edward I.) we read of Sir Robert Lathom and "Thomas de Lathum his grandson." We have here the O. Nor. *hlath* or *hlatha* (dat. pl. *hlathum*)—Dan.-Norw. *lade*, Swed. *lada*—

'storehouse,' 'barn.' *Laith* or *lathe* is a Lancashire dialect-word for 'barn.'[1]

Leigh.—We have a historical record that the leighs or leas (A.-Sax. *leáh*, 'meadowland') in this district are, or were, "green and luxuriant."[2] It is said that the original guttural pronunciation of Leigh is still retained by the natives. West Leigh and Astley (East Leigh) are situated with respect to Leigh exactly as their names imply.

Linacre represents 'the lint or flax field'—A.-Sax. *lin*, 'flax,' 'linen,' and *æcer*, 'field'; O. Nor. *lin-akr*, 'flax field.'

Litherland occurs in Domesday both as *Liderlant* and *Literland*. In the time of King John (1199-1216) we find *Litterland;* of Edward II. (1307-1327), when Norman-French linguistic influence was being considerably weakened, *Lytherland;* and in 1371, *Letherland*. The probable etymology is the O. Nor. *hlithar-land*, 'the sloping land,' which corresponds exactly with the natural aspect of the township. But see under LIVERPOOL.

Lowton was formerly *Lauton*,[3] *i.e.*, the *tún* or settlement by or on a mound or rising ground—A.-Sax. *hlǽw*, 'mound,' 'tumulus,' 'hill.' This word (*hlǽw*) has come down to us in place-names both as *low* and *law*, the latter spelling and pronunciation now being mainly confined to the South of Scotland.[4]

---

[1] Picton, South Lancashire Dialect, *Proceedings* Lit. and Phil. Soc. L'pool, vol. xix. (1864-65), p. 35.
[2] Baines, Lanc., 1870, ii. 203.
[3] Survey of 1320-1346, Chetham Soc., vol. lxxiv., 1868.
[4] This vowel-change is not restricted to Old English. "*Au* is the only diphthong which the Latin language has preserved, that is, in the generality of cases; for here also we find a weakening—to *o*—common in early times. It is observable, however, that the new form in *o* never drove out the old one in *au;* but the two remained side by side. . . . Corssen supposes that *au* was employed by educated men in words where *o* was heard in the mouth of the countryman. This is borne out by the anecdote of Suetonius (*Vespasian*, 22) which Corssen quotes. The homely Emperor was taken to task by the courtier Florus for calling a *plaustrum* (cart) a *plostrum;* and retaliated next day by pronouncing his critic's name as befitted ears so polite—*Flaurus*. . . . Somewhat analogous to the change of sound from *au* to *o* in Latin is the pronunciation of *au* in French; and in some parts of the North of England 'law' is pronounced like *lo*."—Peile, Greek and Latin Etymology, 1869, pp. 154-155.

Lunt or *Lund* here, as in other Danish districts, is referable to the O. Nor. *lund(r)*, 'a sacred grove.' Lunt was therefore the scene of the pagan rites of the ancient Scandinavians who settled in the region.

Lydiate.—This name occurs in Domesday as *Leiate*, which may have meant originally 'the road over the meadow'—A.-Sax. *leáh*, 'lea,' 'meadow'; and *geat*, 'gate,' 'road,' 'passage'; but it is more probable that the name is simply the A.-Sax. *hlidgeat* (Mdle. Eng. *lidgate* or *lidyate*), 'lidgate,' 'postern.' The word is found in some rural districts as 'lidgett' (which is simply a slurred pronunciation of 'lidyate' or 'lydiate'), and in London it appears as Ludgate; in the former case the old palatal pronunciation of *g* (as in 'young' and 'year,' A.-Sax. *geong* and *geár*) being retained, in the latter the guttural (hard) enunciation surviving. We find the spelling *Lydyate* in the Nonarum Inquisitiones (*temp.* Edw. III.), fol. 40ᵇ.

Maghull.—Domesday gives *Magele* as being one of six manors held by the Saxon Uctred before the Conquest. In the Testa de Nevill (fol. 396) the name occurs as *Maghale*. The present spelling is found in 1635. Some have argued (urging the traces of strong Irish influence in the neighbourhood) that the first element of 'Maghull' must be the Gael. *magh*, 'a plain'; but there is little doubt that the *magh* in 'Maghull' is no more of Erse origin than is the equally Gaelic-looking *augh* in 'Aughton,' and that the name should really be divided—taking the Testa de Nevill spelling as affording the best clue to the etymology—as follows : *Mag-hale*, where *hale* (A.-Sax. *healh*, O. Nor. *hallr*) is the common topographic suffix meaning 'a slope.' Maghull is situate on the only rising ground in the immediate neighbourhood. A personal appellation is frequently found prefixed to English place-names ending with mutated forms of *healh* or *hallr*, but in such cases we invariably have clear traces of the genitive (possessive) *s* or *n*, which is entirely lacking in 'Maghull.' A connection with the common A.-Sax. *mǽg* or *maga*, 'son,' 'descendant,' 'kinsman,' is, however, within the bounds of possibility.

Although, as I have said, I discard the notion of the name Maghull being of Erse origin, it is nevertheless interesting to note that the place was "formerly often called *Mail* or *Male*,"¹ a circumstance which is in agreement with Irish phonetics, in which *gh*, under certain conditions, is mute. The spelling *Mael*, too, occurs in a well-known Lancashire record of the first half of the fourteenth century.² Now when we recollect that *mael* is Old Irish³ for 'a bald or bare hill,'⁴ it seems hard to resist the inference that ' Maghull ' is of Erse origin. But it is quite clear that, while a *Mael* might result from a *Maghull*, a *Maghull* could not possibly result from an original *Mael*. The old Irish plantation influence in the district, already mentioned, was evidently responsible for the Hibernicising of the *Magele* of Domesday and the *Maghale* of the Testa de Nevill into *Mael*.

Makerfield.—The first portion of this name has much tested the resources of etymologists, and little wonder, considering the variation in spelling which it has undergone in the course of its career—*Macerfeld*, *Maserfelth*, *Maresfeld*, *Maxsefeld*, etc. An unlikely derivation put forward a long time ago was from the Gael. *magh*, 'a plain.' I do not remember to have seen the A.-Sax. *mæger* (O. Nor. *magr*, Lat. *macer*, Eng. *meagre*), 'lean,' 'poor,' 'barren,' advanced. The Swedes have the expressions *mager jord*, 'poor or barren soil,' and *mager åker*, ' a sterile field '; while Cicero connected *macer* with *solum*, indicating ' poor soil.' We must recollect that the A.-Sax. and Ger. *feld* originally denoted a place where trees had been *felled*. Local antiquaries identify Makerfield with the Maserfelth where Oswald, king of the Northumbrians, was slain in battle with Penda, king of the Mercians, in 642, as related by the Venerable Bede; but this is not allowed in general history. Stevenson, referring to the conflict, says : " Although a place near Winwick, in Lancashire, named Maserfield, has claims to be regarded as the spot where this battle was fought, yet there are much stronger arguments in favour of Oswestry (*i.e.*, 'Oswald's Tree '), in Shropshire."⁵ And Plummer, the latest editor of

---

¹ Baines, Lanc., 1870, ii. 425.
² Survey of 1320-1346, Chetham Soc., vol. lxxiv., 1868.
³ Modern Irish and Gaelic have the form *maol* (Welsh, *moel*), *ao* being a modern aphthong substituted for the older *ae* and *oe*.
⁴ Joyce, Irish Local Names Explained, 1884, p. 104.
⁵ Bede's Historia Ecclesiastica, Stevenson's ed., 1841, i. 177.

Bede, equating Maserfelth with Oswestry, makes no mention of the claims of the Lancashire Makerfield.[1] The student of battle-sites should not, however, omit to note Mr. Browne's 'Pre-Norman Sculptured Stones in Lancashire,' in the *Transactions* of the Lancashire and Cheshire Antiquarian Society, vol. v., 1887. The Welsh name of Oswestry is *Croes* [cross] *Oswallt*.

Melling.—The Domesday spelling is *Melinge*. At first sight we would appear to have here a pure Anglo-Saxon patronymic; but there is little doubt that 'Melling' is a Saxonisation of the name of the Norman, Vivian de Molines, to whom, shortly after the Conquest, Roger de Poictou granted a large tract of land in this district. The Molyneux family trace their descent from William des Molines, so named from Moulins ('the Mills'), a town of Bourbonnais in France. The historical gradation in the spelling of this family name is as follows: Molines, Molynes, Moulins, Mulans, Mulynes, Mulyneus, Molineux, Molyneux.

Mersey.—The circumstance that the Mersey, unlike the Dee, the Severn, the Thames, and other English rivers, does not seem to bear a Celtic name, was once thought to confirm a widely-accepted theory that within historic times the Dee and the Mersey had but one estuary between them, and that certain defined depressions of the Wirral peninsula once conveyed the superfluous waters of the Mersey into the then larger volume of the sister river. The Belisama of Ptolemy, after a protracted controversy, was concluded to be the Ribble, and, there apparently being a lack of reference to the Mersey during the Roman sway in this country, it was estimated, seeing that the Danes and Norsemen sailed up the river, that the Mersey must have cut itself an independent outlet to the sea, by way of what is now Liverpool, between the fifth and eighth centuries. But Mr. T. G. Rylands, F.S.A., who, originally instigated by a friend's interrogation as to whether the Belisama was the Mersey or the Ribble (the Editors of the 'Monumenta Historica Britannica,' 1848, gave both), devoted almost a

---

[1] Bede's Historia Ecclesiastica, Plummer's ed., 1896, i. 451, ii. 494.

lifetime to the study of Ptolemy, has conclusively proved[1] that the Belisama can only be the Mersey.

Mr. Rylands's researches into Ptolemy's geography of our north-western coast may be summed up as follows:

Ianganorum Prom.	=	Brachypwll.
Tisobius	=	Traeth Mawr.
Seteia	=	Dee.
Belisama	=	Mersey.
Setantiorum Portus	=	Ribble.
Ituna	=	Solway.

In Domesday the Mersey figures as *Mersha* ('Inter Ripam et Mersham'). The earliest Saxon document mentioning the Mersey which has so far been found is the will of Wulfric Spott, which was confirmed by King Ethelred in 1004. This Wulfric was a Mercian nobleman, a large landowner (even for those times), and the founder of the Abbey of Burton-on-Trent. He bequeathed to his sons Ælfhelm and Wulfag, *inter alia*, the lands "betwux Ribbel and *Mærse* and on Wirhalum." The will was printed by Sir William Dugdale,[2] with a Latin translation and an identification-list of the place-names mentioned in it. Sir Francis Palgrave[3] describes the testament as "a singular and important document requiring much topographical and legal illustration." He adds that "Dugdale's translation is not particularly accurate," a term which might also be applied to Sir William's transcription of the will.

It is worth remembering that just as we have a Wallasea (island) on the coast of Essex, so have we a Mersea[4] (island)

---

[1] Ptolemy Elucidated, 1893, *passim*. The broad results of his elaborate investigations had, however, long previously been published, *viz.*, in the *Transactions* Hist. Soc. Lanc. and Chesh.: Ptolemy's Geography of the Coast from Carnarvon to Cumberland, 1877-78, pp. 81 *sqq.*, and The Map-History of the Coast from the Dee to the Duddon, 1878-79, pp. 83 *sqq.*

[2] Monasticon Anglicanum, 1682, i. 266: ed. 1817-30, iii. 37.

[3] Rise and Progress of the English Commonwealth: Anglo-Saxon Period, 1832, ii. 293.

[4] This is the island mentioned in the entry in the Saxon Chronicle under A.D. 895, which describes how, in this year, the Danish army departed from Wirheal (Wirral) into N. Wales, marching thence across Northumbria and East Anglia (striving to avoid Alfred's forces) into Essex, finally taking up their quarters on Mersea—"oth that hie

there. *Mersea* (A.-Sax. *Meres-ig*) has been explained as 'the sea island,' and *Mersey*, by analogy, as 'the sea river.' The latter interpretation, at least, is illogical. The A.-Sax. *mere* (1) 'sea' (2) 'lake,' 'pool,' 'mere,'[1] there is little doubt, is the base of both names; but, in my opinion, it must here be translated 'pool' or 'lake,' not 'sea,' as, for example, in Alfred's interpolation of 'The Voyages of Ohthere and Wulfstan' in his translation of Orosius, where he speaks of "swíthe micle meras" (very large meres) throughout "thá móras" (the moors). The low-lying lands at the mouth of and in the estuary of the Mersey, have, from time immemorial, like the flat coast of Essex, been subject to inundations, with the natural result of the formation of meres and marshes (A.-Sax. *mersc*, for *merisc*, lit. 'mere-ish'). And I believe the *s* in both 'Mersey' and 'Mersea' may represent not the genitive singular but the nominative plural case, which, although (as we have just seen) *as* in the classic West Saxon, was, like the gen. sing., *es* in the Dano-Saxon dialects. 'Mersey' would therefore correspond to an original *Meres-eá*, just as 'Mersea' represents an original *Meres-ig*—A.-Sax. *eá*, O. Nor. *á*, 'river,' 'water;' A.-Sax. *ig* (form of *eá*), O. Nor. *ey*, 'island.' It will be seen that to be quite regular the Essex Mersea and the Lancashire and Cheshire Mersey should be reversed in spelling.

Whitaker, the historian of Manchester, 120 years ago, was within reasonable distance of what we must accept as the true etymology of 'Mersey.' Reading *Mærsc* (instead of *Mærse*) as the name of the river in the will of Wulfric, he remarks: "from the marshes and marshy meadows that skirt its channel on both sides, in one continued line to the

---

cómon on Eástseaxna land eásteweard on án ígland thæt is úte on thére sǽ, thæt is *Meresig* háten." This part of the Chronicle dealing with Alfred's campaigns against the Danes Dr. Sweet describes (Anglo-Saxon Reader, 1894, p. 35) as "a perfect model of Old English prose," while Prof. Earle considers it to be "the most remarkable piece of writing in the whole series of Chronicles." In Ethelwerd's Chronicle (*lib.* iiii.) the Essex Mersea is referred to as "a place in Kent"!—"ad Meresige locum Cantiam" (*sic*).

[1] The A.-Sax. *mere* has not come down to our day in its original form without undergoing metaplasm in the interval. For example, Levins's Manipulus Vocabulorum, 1570 (printed by the Early Eng. Text Soc.), has the epenthetic form *meare*.

sea, obtaining the descriptive denomination of Mersc-ey, Mers-ey, or marshy water."[1]

A word may be added as to the conceivability of the first element of 'Mersey' being a relic of Celtic nomenclature. At first sight there does not appear to be much in common between Belisama and Mersey; but a phonological examination of the name which Ptolemy probably wrote down from the lips of Roman or Greek sailors may perhaps induce us to take a contrary view. The most noticeable point to begin with is the occurrence of *s* in the middle of both Belisama and Mersey. Turning then to the first letter of Ptolemy's name, *b*, phonologists well know that this is readily mutable to both *v* and *m*, and conversely.[2] *E* is the second letter in both names. Then we have *l* in Belisama and *r* in Mersey. This presents no difficulty; *l* and *r*, both liquids, are or have been interchangeable in many languages, the greater tendency being for *r* to slide into the easier-sounded *l*.[3] The dual occurrence of medial *s* having already been noted, this, of course, is as far as the comparison can be taken. The apparent similarities may only be coincidental, but it is at any rate just conceivable that the Saxons might transform, say, a Celtic Marusia ('dead water'), a name which possessed no meaning for them, into *Mcres-ca*, which was full of significance to them. But, after all, this is pure conjecture.

From a work entirely devoted to the Mersey, like Dr. Blower's,[4] we might have expected some treatment of the

---

[1] Hist. of Manchester, 1775, ii. 238.

[2] See Peile, Greek and Latin Etymology, 1869, pp. 234, 235, and Max Müller, Science of Language, 2nd ser., 1864, p. 145; compare the Welsh mutations—*e.g. bara*, 'bread'; *dy fara* (vara), 'thy bread'; *fy mara*, 'my bread'; the Irish *b*, *m* = *v* or *w*; Mod. Gr. β = *v*, Lat. *Sabrina* = Severn, Lat. *Abona* = Avon, etc.; and note, in our own language, 'somersault,' from Fr. *soubresaut*; 'malmsey,' from Fr. *malvoisie*; 'marble,' prim. from Lat. *marmor*.

[3] Peile, Greek and Latin Etymology, 1869, p. 81; Max Müller, Science of Language, 2nd ser., 1864, pp. 165, 166; Morris, Historical English Grammar, 1875, p. 44, etc. Eng. 'palfrey' is ultimately from Low Lat. *paraveredus*; 'chapter,' conversely, from Lat. *capitulum*; 'Gibraltar' is a corruption of *Gibel-al-Tarik*. The Chinaman is perhaps the greatest adult sufferer from lallation or lambdacism. In his mouth 'America' becomes *Melika*.

[4] Mersey, Ancient and Modern, by Benj. Blower, 1878.

name, but I can find nothing in the book beyond a literal reproduction from Baines of an untenable etymological connection with 'Mercia,' which Sir Peter Leycester seems to have suggested originally: speaking of the great Midland kingdom this Cestrian chronicler said:[1] "It was called Mercia, not from the river Mersey running from the corner of Wirral, in Cheshire, because that river was the utmost limit thereof westward; but I rather believe that river took denomination from this kingdom, which it bounded on that side, and was called Mercia, because it abutted or bordered upon part of all or most of the other kingdoms of the Heptarchy."

Netherton.— Anglo-Saxon: 'the lower enclosure or farmstead'—A.-Sax. *neothor*, 'lower.'

Newsham.—This name now survives only in Newsham Park and Newsham House. In the Testa de Nevill it is spelt *Neusum* (fol. 403) and *Neusom* (fol. 409), forms which point to an original A.-Sax. *Niwehúsum*, 'at the new houses,' *húsum* being the dative plural of *hús*, 'house.' Other English Newshams figure in Domesday as *Newehusun*, *Newhuson*, etc.; and the Durham Newsham appears in the Boldon Book as *Newsom*.

Newton is the *Neweton* of Domesday—A.-Sax. *niwe*, 'new.' The primary signification of A.-Sax. *tún* was 'enclosure'; then it naturally came to mean 'farm' or 'manor'; and the name *tún* was retained when, in process of time, a village grew up round the farm. There are several scores of Newtons in England, and it is probable that our Newton, like most of the rest, simply denotes the spot where a Saxon cultivator had taken up a new estate; but Dr. Robson, the Warrington antiquary, had a much less prosaic theory of the origin of the name. He says that, on the death of King Oswald, the traditionary site of whose palace, and of the well, is at Wood End, near Hermitage Green, "the royal residence seems to have been transferred to another site to which naturally enough the name of Newton, the new town or *vill*, was given."[2]

[1] Antiquities of Cheshire, 1673, p. 92.
[2] Transactions Hist. Soc. Lanc. and Chesh., 1851-52, p. 205.

North Meols.—In Domesday we have *Mele*. This name is referable to the O. Nor. *melr* (genit. *mels*, pl. *melar*), 'sand-hill,' ' sand-bank.'

Orford.—' The cattle-ford '—A.-Sax. *orf*, ' cattle '; and *ford*.

Ormskirk does not figure in Domesday, but the first settled possession of the ancient parish, and the establishment of the kirk, are ascribed by local historians to a Northman bearing the common name Orm—O. Nor. *ormr*, 'serpent.'

Orrell.—'Orrell' is all that has come down to us of the name of a place which in Domesday is chronicled as *Otegrimele*. In the last element of the ancient designation we have, of course, the O. Nor. *melr* (pl. *melar*, genit. sing. *mels*), 'a stretch of sand.' *O* and *U* are the Scandinavian negative particles. Thus, in Swedish, *täck* is 'agreeable,' *otäck* is 'nasty.' It is probable that *otäck* or its etymon has nothing to do with *Otegri*; but there is an O. Nor. word *teigr*, ' a strip of field or meadow-land '; and, as Cleasby (' Icelandic Dict.') has pointed out, the use of the Icelandic negative prefix *ú* or *ó* is almost unlimited. The hypothesis, therefore—I give it for lack of a better—is that Orrell represented roughly, originally, ' the sandy area out of which not a strip of meadow-land could be got.' Another Orrell, in Sefton parish, is set down in Domesday as *Otringemele*.

Padgate.—' The path-gate '—A.-Sax. *pæð-geat*.

Parr.—This name was formerly spelled *Parre*. A parr (etymology dubious) is a young salmon ; but it is of course impossible to connect this fish with Parr. The name is probably a diminution of A.-Sax. *parruc* or *pearroc* (Scot. *parrok*, Eng. *parrock*), ' croft,' ' enclosure,' 'park.' Compare Mdle. Eng. *parren*, ' to enclose ' ; *parred*, ' enclosed.' This etymology would seem to be confirmed by a note in Mr. Way's edition of a celebrated 15th cent. vocabulary[1] under *parrok—viz* : " In Norfolk, according to Forby, an enclosed place for domestic animals, as calves, is called a par, and the farmyard, containing pars for the various animals which inhabit it, is called a par-yard."

[1] Promptorium Parvulorum, Camden Soc., ii. (1853) 384.

Pemberton.—There is no name resembling Pemberton to be found in the Testa de Nevill; but the place is mentioned, spelt as it is to-day, in the Survey of 1320-1346, Chetham Soc., vol. lxxiv., 1868. Despite the scantiness of early information as to the name—a fault not uncommon with Lancashire place-appellations compared with those of the more fertile, earlier-settled, and consequently anciently more thickly peopled counties of the South, East, and West of England—there is little difficulty in coming to the conclusion that the original Anglo-Saxon name was *Pín-bearu-tún*, 'the pine-grove farmstead.' Compare Pamber Forest in the South of England.

Penketh.—This name has apparently suffered much curtailment and assimilation in the course of centuries, and little beyond a more or less reasonable guess can be made as to its full original meaning. The earliest spelling recorded seems to be that in the Testa de Nevill (fol. 396), *viz.*, *Penket*, where the dropping of the present-day final *h* does not necessarily mean that the name was pronounced as spelt by any but Norman-French scribes.

Penketh, however, occurs in the Survey of 1320-1346, Chetham Soc., vol. lxxiv., 1868. The last three letters in Penketh may represent, as they do in Lambeth (Lamb-hithe) the Anglo-Saxon *hýth*, 'hithe,' 'haven,' 'landing-place';[1] while the first element of the name may be a mutilated patronymic, or even refer to a (silver) penny rental—A.-Sax. *pening* (penny). We can imagine how easily *Pen(n)ing-hýth* (or the genit. pl. *Pen(n)inga-hýth*) could eventually be corrupted into 'Penketh.' On the other hand, as there is a heath close to the township (at any rate, there is one marked on the last Ordnance map of the district) it is not impossible that *eth* may represent the A.-Sax. *hǽth* (heath). There are no physiographical or general grounds for Canon Taylor's classification ('Words and Places,' 3rd ed., 1873, p. 147) of Penketh with place-names associated with the Welsh *pen*, 'headland.'

A Cymric origin can, however, it may be interesting to note for purposes of comparison, be claimed for Penkridge

---

[1] This might seem to be borne out by the spelling *Penkythe*, which is found in the Calendarium Inquisitionum Post Mortem, ii. (*temp.* Edw. III.) 238.

in Staffordshire. The ancient name was *Pennocrucium*, which Professor Rhys, perhaps our chief Celticist, explains as follows:[1] "*penno-s*, 'head' or 'top'; *crūcio*, which became in Welsh *crūc*, now *crūg*, a 'heap' or 'mound'; the whole would mean the top or head of the mound or barrow."

Pennington was the *tún* or settlement of the Saxon Penning family.[2] Occasionally, however, a place-name with *Penning* may have reference to a rental. Thus Penninghame, near Newton-Stewart, is said to be a ham or piece of land which was held at a charge of a silver penny (A.-Sax. *pening*).

Poulton.—'The farmstead by the pool'—A.-Sax. *pul*, 'pool'; *tún*, 'farmstead,' 'manor.'

Prescot. — 'The priest's dwelling' — A.-Sax. *preóst*, 'priest,' and *cot*, 'cottage.' According to tradition Prescot "was anciently the habitation of priests."

Rainford is a corruption of *Randleford*, Randle being the name of a brook running through the village.[3]

Rainhill.—In the Survey of 1320-1346, Chetham Soc., vol. lxxiv., 1868, we have the spelling *Raynhull*. In the early part of the 15th century *Raynhill* occurs. The name may be a corruption of A.-Sax. *hræfn-hyll*, 'raven-hill,' or possibly an assimilation of some personal appellation (Rainham in Kent was originally *Roegingaham*); but the former theory is the more feasible. The raven was the war-emblem of the ancient Danes, and Raven Hill, in Whitby parish, N. Yorks, obtained its name from the Danes having set up their standard upon it after landing in 867. There is, moreover, a village called Ravenhead within a short distance of Rainhill. But, on the whole, I am inclined to think that the first element of the name is nothing more than the Northern dialect-word *rain*, 'ridge,' 'balk,' etc.—O. Nor. *rein* (*cf*. Ger. *rain*) 'strip of land'—in

---

[1] Celtic Britain, 1884, p. 303.
[2] Birch's ed. (1876) of Kemble's Saxons in England, i. 470.
[3] Rev. J. Bridger to the author.

allusion to the old method of cultivating the hill, *viz.*, separating the ploughed portions by rains, *i.e.*, ridges or balks.[1]

Ravensmeols.—The name of this Scandinavian settlement occurred in Domesday as *Erengermeles*, the latter portion of which is the usual O. Nor. *melr* (genit. case *mels*), pl. *melar*, 'sand-hills' or 'sand-banks'; while the front part of the name may be referable to the O. Nor. *eyrr* (Dan. *öre*, Swed. *ör*) 'a gravel bank' (of a river or of small tongues of land running into the sea), and the O. Nor. *eng* or *engi*, pl. *engiar*, 'meadows,' the name, upon this hypothesis, meaning 'the gravel meadow strips among the banks or hills of sand.' This is, of course, presuming that the name recorded in the Norman Survey is an approximately correct rendering of the native appellation, which may otherwise have embodied a personal name, the raven (O. Nor. *hrafn*, Dan. *ravn*) being the war-emblem of the ancient Danes.

Risley was 'the brushwood pasture'—A.-Sax. *hris*, 'brushwood'; *leáh*, 'pasture'; or, perhaps, as Risley borders upon the large moss of that name, 'the rushy meadow'—A.-Sax. *risc*, 'rush.'

Rixton.—The spelling is the same in the Testa de Nevill. This was 'the farmstead by the rushes'—A.-Sax. *rix*, *risc*, 'rush'; *tún*, 'farmstead,' 'manor.'

Roby.—Domesday spelling *Rabil*. The name of this village is practically identical with that of Raby on the opposite side of the Mersey, the *Rabil* of the Norman Survey "Inter Ripam et Mersham" doubtless being a copyist's mistake for *Rabie*,[2] the spelling which figures in the Cheshire Domesday. In both 'Roby' and 'Raby' we probably have, prefixed to the usual Scand. word for 'settlement,' 'village'—*by*—the animal-name of the original Scandinavian owner of the settlement, the O. Nor. *rá*, pron. as *row* = noise—Dan.-Norw. *raa*, Swed. *rå*, both pron. *raw*—meaning 'a roe.' This animal-name was borne by more than one member of the royal family of ancient Denmark.

---

[1] See Note, p. 45; also Halliwell, Dict. of Archaic and Provincial English, 1850; and Seebohm, English Village Community, 1884, p. 381.

[2] *Raby* occurs in The Great de Lacy Inquisition of February 16, 1311, Chetham Soc., vol. lxxiv., 1868.

Sankey.—Some of the old spellings found of this name are: *Sanki, Sanky, Sanchi, Sonky, Sankye, Sonkey, Sanckey,* and *Sonkie.* All these seem to point to one signification: 'the sunken (or low) place by the water'—A.-Sax. *sencan* (pret. sing. *sanc*), 'to sink'; *ig* (*iy*) primarily 'island,' but also indicating low riparian land.

Mr. Beamont[1] mentions the absurd derivation "from the words 'sand' and 'quay'"; and I can trace no historical grounds for his alternative etymology, "the Sank, the brook which goes through the place, with the *ey* or *eyot* at its mouth."

In some 'Notes on the Local, Natural, and Geological History of Rainhill,'[2] by the Rev. H. H. Higgins, M.A., occurs the following passage: "Rainhill was then part of an island, or rather of a peninsula; all the flat lands of Speke and Ditton were under the sea, which swept round far to the east of Rainhill, leaving Appleton and Bold high and dry, but pouring its waters over the Sankey Brook district.... This was the condition of things probably not so very long ago, I mean since the appearance of man upon the earth, though how many thousands of years ago it would be a mere guess to suggest."

Scarisbrick.—In an Inspeximus of 17 Edward II. (1324) contained in the chartulary of Burscough, a charter without date is cited in which occurs the name "Walter, lord of *Scaresbrek.*" We meet with *Scaresbreck* in 1508, and with *Scarisbrick* about the middle of the 17th century. The ancient spellings imply 'the slope-land belonging to one Scar or Skardh'—O. Nor. *brekka,* 'a slope.' As a personal appellation the O. Nor. *skardh,* 'a gap or cut in a rock,' meant 'hare-lip.' *Skardh* or *Skardhi* was a frequent Danish proper name on the Runic stones ('Scarborough' is derived therefrom), and *brekka* figures frequently in Icelandic local names.

Seaforth.—This modern residential suburb is an instance, with Liverpool and Hoylake, of a township bearing the name of a sheet of water; the present appellation being borrowed by Mr. Gladstone's father from the Scottish

---

[1] Hist. of Sankey, 1889, p. 1.
[2] *Proceedings* Lit. and Phil. Soc., L'pool, vol. xxi. (1866-67), p. 64.

Seaforth, which is derived from the O. Nor. *sær* (accus. *sæ*), 'sea,' and *fiörthr*, 'firth,' 'frith,' 'bay.'

Sephton or **Sefton**.—Domesday has *Sextone* ; the Valor of Pope Nicholas (1291) *Cefton* ; the Testa de Nevill, *Ceffton*.

The Rev. Geo. W. Wall, Rector of Sephton, writes to me: "Up to the death of a rector in the sixteenth century, 'Sefton' obtains in the registers ; but his burial is entered as 'of Sephton,' and 'Sephton,' with few exceptions, is the ecclesiastical spelling thenceforward, and is engraved on the church plate, etc. . . . 'Sephton' appears the later use. . . . I do not think that the Lancashire and Cheshire Historical Society . . . have ever attempted a derivation."

Unless the *Sextone* of Domesday is a clerical error, it might imply that the original farmstead was *Seaf's tún*. We find this name, combined with the patronymic suffix *ing*, in such English village names as Scavington and Sevington. On the other hand, the designation of the township under discussion occurs so consistently in post-Domesday times without a medial genitive *s*, that it seems impossible to reject the conclusion that *Sextone* is a blunder of a Norman scribe, and that the name must be referable to the O. Nor. *sef* (Swed. *säf*, Dan.-Norw. *siv*, A.-Sax. *secg*), 'sedge.' This definition would be accurately borne out by the natural characteristics of the district, which is low and swampy. We find the word *sef* in such Icelandic local names as *sef-dæla*, 'sedgy hollow,' *sef-tjörn*, 'sedge-tarn.'

Skelmersdale.—Uctred, at the time of the Domesday Survey, held *Schelmeresdele*. The literal meaning of the name is 'the devil's dale'—O. Nor. *skelmir* (genit. sing. *skelmis*), 'devil'; but *Skelmir* was doubtless the name of the original Scandinavian proprietor.

Southport received its name in a somewhat arbitrary fashion at a dinner which a Mr. Sutton, of North Meols, gave in 1792, in celebration of his founding a hotel on the site of the now favourite watering-place.

Southworth.—The latter element of this name is the A.-Sax. *weorthig*, 'farm,' 'estate.'

Speke.—*Spec* is the Domesday rendering. There is only one Speke in England. The name may possibly be referred to the A.-Sax. *spǽc-hús*, 'a court hall'—*spǽc*, 'speech'; *hús*, 'house,' 'hall'—hence the famous Speke Hall;[1] but it is more probable that it is the A.-Sax. *spic* (Ger. *speck*), which, as Kemble points out,[2] properly signifying 'bacon,' was used to denote swine pastures.

Spellow.—Anciently *Spellawe*. In the second element we have the common A.-Sax. *hlǽw*, 'hill,' 'mound' (as in *Low* Hill); the first syllable in names formed similarly to this (for example, Spelhoe in Northants) is generally ascribed to the A.-Sax. *spell*, 'speech,' Spellow thus meaning Speech-hill.

St. Helen's derives its name from the old episcopal chapel of St. Helen—called St. Ellen in 1650.

Stanley.—The name of this Liverpool suburb is derived from the noble family bearing that patronymic, which signifies 'the stony or rocky meadow'—A.-Sax. *stán*, 'stone,' 'rock'; *leáh*, 'meadow,' 'lea'—and is ultimately to be referred to Staffordshire. "The family of Stanley is a branch of the ancient barons of Audeley or Aldelegh, in Staffordshire, one of whom, Adam, had two sons, Lydulph and Adam. The former, Lydulph de Aldelegh (*temp.* Stephen), was progenitor of the barons Audeley: the second son, Adam, assumed the name of Aldithlega or Audleigh, and had a son, William, to whom his uncle Lydulph gave Stanleigh or Stoneleigh, in Staffordshire, on which he assumed the surname of Stanley."[3]   See WINSTANLEY.

Tarbock.—Domesday has *Torboc*. The township takes its name from the local beck or brook, which was anciently known as the *Torbec*, that is, 'the stream of (the Scandinavian deity) Tor, or Thor'—O. Nor. *bekkr*, Dan. *bæk*, Swed. *bäck*, 'brook.'

Thingwall.—"Between the parishes of Childwall and West Derby, but included in neither of them," say the

---
[1] In later times the 'speke-house' was the parlour or reception-room of a convent.
[2] Codex Diplomaticus, iii. xxxvii.
[3] Baines, Lanc., 1870, ii. 271.

editors of Baines's 'Lancashire' (1870, ii. 387), "lies the hamlet of Thingwall. Being extra-parochial, and now consisting of a single estate, and without any dwellings on it except the mansion of the proprietor, and an old farm or manor-house, it seems to have escaped the notice of topographers, is unnoticed in the census returns, and received no mention whatever in the original edition of this work; yet it gave a surname to an ancient family, and is mentioned as a distinct manor in the early 'extents' and 'inquisitions' of the county, while its name affords one of the most distinct traces of the early settlement of this part of the county by Scandinavian invaders."

This Thingwall (O. Nor. *thing*, 'parliament,' *völlr* (dat. case *velli*), 'field') undoubtedly marks the spot at which the Norsemen of south-west Lancashire were accustomed to meet in council, promulgate decrees, and transact other business of importance, just as the Thingwall in Cheshire was the parliament-field of the Wirral Norsemen; while Tynwald is the parliament-field in the Isle of Man to this day. The name occurs, more or less disguised, in other portions of the country which were settled by the Danes and Norsemen. The modern Norwegian *stor-t(h)ing* is 'the great court' or 'parliament.' It seems to have been the aim of the Scandinavians in choosing a *thingvöllr* to select a plain in the middle of which rose an eminence upon which the chief men could take their stand and address the people upon the lower levels around them. It is thus that in some cases the Norse name *thingvöllr* or 'thingwall' eventually came to denote the eminence alone instead of the flat expanse around it.

The Lancashire Thingwall is not mentioned in Domesday, but the chief manor of Derbei Hundred is recorded in that Survey as containing six berewicks, or subordinate manors, and it is considered that Thingwall was one of these.

Thornton.—The ash, the oak, and the thorn (A.-Sax. *porn*) have supplied the bulk of English place-names derived from plant-life. The various Thorntons are frequently represented in Domesday, as in this instance, by *Torentun*. The Lancashire Thornton occurs in the Testa de Nevill as *Thorinton*.

Toxteth.—This name occurs in Domesday as *Stochestede*, i.e., 'the stockaded or enclosed place'—A.-Sax. *stocc* (Ger. *stock*), 'stake'; A.-Sax. *stede* (Ger. *stadt*), 'place,' 'stead.'

Tuebrook is the name of a small stream which has given a designation to a residential district of Liverpool. The late Sir J. A. Picton thought he detected a Celtic word meaning 'muddy' in the first syllable[1]; but it is probable that, as 'brook' is Anglo-Saxon (*bróc*), so also is 'Tue'— doubtless Tiw, the god of war, as in 'Tuesday,' A.-Sax. *Tiwes-dæg*. 'Tuebrook' is therefore a variant of 'Thorburn,' where the latter does not represent the Norse heroic personal name Thorbiörn (*biörn* = bear).

Tyldesley.—In the printed Testa de Nevill the name of this township occurs as *Tyldisley*, *Tyldesley*, and *Tydesley* on fol. 396, and as *Tydesle* thrice on fol. 398[b]. It is impossible from the known existing documentary evidence to say which spelling is nearest the original form, or whether the first *l* in the present-day form and in some of the earlier spellings is or is not an epenthetic intrusion, due merely to a rustic assimilative pronunciation, somewhat, perhaps, in the way that *Gibel-al-Tarik* was ultimately resolved into Gibraltar. Were the first *l* really intrusive, the name would probably have an affinity with the Derbyshire Tideswell. In any case the first element is most likely a personal appellation. We could scarcely connect the A.-Sax. *tilð* (genit. *tilðes*), 'tilth,' 'cultivation,' etc. (from *tilian*, 'to till'), with a ley or meadow.

Upholland, near Wigan, occurs in Domesday as *Hoiland*, and there is no doubt that, as in the case of Downholland, this name is referable to an original A.-Sax. *Holt-land*, 'wood-land.' Upholland lies much higher than its antithesis, Downholland; hence the later prefix; and it is still contiguous to woods. See DOWNHOLLAND.

Walton.—The Domesday form is *Waletone*. There are many Waltons in England, and as a rule we have to distinguish whether the name was applied to a walled *tún* or settlement (A.-Sax. *weall*, 'wall') or to an enclosure

---

[1] Memorials of Liverpool, i. 4.

hemmed in by a weald (A.-Sax. *weald*, Ger. *wald*) or wood. There is, I think, no difficulty here: "In 33 Edward I. [1305] William de Waleton impleaded Robert Byroun and forty-six defendants for cutting down oak and other trees growing in Waleton, under the pretext that the townships of Waleton and Kyrkeby were united by a wood in which they had the privilege of husbote."[1]

Wargrave.—This name has troubled topographic philologists as to both its elements. C. Blackie[2] does not mention it; but the untrustworthy Edmunds[3] glosses it as 'the ditch enclosure.' *War* has been variously taken to represent E. Eng. *werre*, 'war,' A.-Sax. *wær*, 'sea,' A.-Sax. *wár*, 'seaweed,' A.-Sax. *waroth*, 'shore,' A.-Sax. *waru*, 'defence,' A.-Sax. *wyrt*, 'wort,' O. Nor. *ver*, or A.-Sax. *wer*, 'fishing-station,' O. Nor. *vörr*, 'landing-place,' and even A.-Sax. *wer*, 'man'; while *grave* has generally been thought to be A.-Sax. *græf* (grave), presumed to mean 'ditch,' or 'trench'; but the Fr. *grève*, 'strand,' has also been mentioned. Study of this and somewhat similar names leads me to think that 'Wargrave' indicates 'the grove by the fishing-station'—A.-Sax. *wer*, 'weir,' 'dam,' 'fish-trap,' 'fish-pond'; A.-Sax. *gráf*, 'grove.' Ware, on the Lea, is the spot where the Danes raised a great weir, or dam. Wareham (anc. *Werham*), in Dorsetshire, was defined by Lewis, in his "Topographical Dictionary,' as 'the habitation on the fishing shore.' It is, however, not impossible that 'Wargrave' may in some instance represent an original A.-Sax. *wír-gráf*, 'myrtle grove.'

Warrington.—Apart from the Domesday rendering, *Walintune*, which is probably an error, the earliest-found spelling of the name of this town is in a document estimated to be of the end of the twelfth century, which has *Werington*, i.e., the *tún* or settlement of the Wærings, members of which clan also held estates at Werrington in Devonshire and Northampton, Wehringen and Weringhausen in Germany, and perhaps at Varengreville in Normandy.

---

[1] Baines, Lanc., 1870, ii. 284.
[2] Dict. of Place-names, 3rd ed., 1887.
[3] Names of Places, 2nd ed., 1872, p. 307.

Waterloo.—Where it is indigenous, this place name simply means 'the watery lea or meadow.' In the case of the interesting Liverpool suburb it presents no etymological significance. The place barely existed in 1835, and ultimately rose into being round a hostelry called the Waterloo Hotel. After Wellington's victory over Napoleon, the name Waterloo became very popular, one of the principal bridges over the Thames being christened from the Belgian battleplace.

Wavertree.—Domesday has *Wavretreu;* but the place has also been anciently styled *Wartre, Waudter, Wave, Wavre,* and even *Wastpull* and *Wastyete.* The editors of Baines's 'Lancashire' (1870, ii. 267) were of the opinion that "All these forms of the name bear unanimous testimony to the barren, uncultivated nature of the district—Wastyete, or Wastgate, the gate or road over the waste; Wastpull, the pool on the waste; of both of which there are remains to this day in the village green and the pool. There is not a doubt that, until within a recent period, a great part of Wavertree and the neighbourhood was unenclosed and consequently uncultivated. So recently as 1769, on Yates's map of the country round Liverpool, Childwall Heath stretched from Wavertree to Woolton."

It is, however, manifestly incorrect to say that "*all* these forms of the name bear unanimous testimony to the barren, uncultivated nature of the district." The terms Wastyete and Wastpull can have absolutely nothing to do with Wartre, Waudter, Wavre, etc., and were evidently either simply alternative designations of the district under discussion, or designations of different portions of it; while the latter group of names are clearly corruptions or contractions of the Domesday rendering, *Wavretreu,* which is well preserved in the modern name. Canon Taylor, in his 'Words and Places' (1864, p. 240), classified 'Wavertree' as a Welsh name, and this allocation might have seemed to receive some confirmation from the fact that a lithic circle was discovered here, which has been thought to be Druidic; but the common Southern Celtic *tre,* 'village,' is invariably a prefix in accord with the genius of the Celtic tongues;[1] and

---

[1] " In this township are found traces of very ancient inhabitants in the Calder-stones, a small circle of diminutive monoliths on the S.E.

in his later work, 'Names and their Histories' (1896, p. 377), the Canon has wisely transferred the name to the simple English 'tree' class. As to the probable meaning of the first element of 'Wavertree,' I cannot, perhaps, do better than quote a note which I have received from Professor Skeat. "Chaucer," he says, "has *wipple-tree* for the cornel-tree, meaning 'waving-tree,' and the A.-Sax. *wæfer* = always on the move, vibrating. And *waver-tree* would be a splendid word for an aspen."

West Derby.—The mediæval importance of this place (Domesday, *Derbei*) is well testified by its giving a name to one of the six hundreds of Lancashire. The midland Derby, from which the Lancashire Derby has been distinguished by the addition of the prefix West, occurs in the Saxon Chronicle as *Deoraby*, and it has been usual to consider both places as being originally 'the location of wild animals'—O. Nor. *dȳr* (A.-Sax. *deór*—whence Eng. *deer*—Ger. *thier*), '(wild) beast,' combined with the customary Scandinavian 'settlement' or 'village' suffix, *bȳ(r)*, a derivation which is not inconceivable, so far as the Lancashire township is concerned, when we call to mind the forestral nature of the district in olden times, and recollect that (West) Dyrby, or Derby, seems to have been used as a kind of centre at which hunting expeditions were organized; but it is, nevertheless, not improbable, considering how many English *bys* have a personal appellation as their prefix, that (West) Derby may have been given the name of its founder.

---

boundary of the township, and in the sepulchral remains which were disinterred in 1867 by the men engaged to excavate the foundations of two houses in Victoria Park. These remains consisted of eight cinerary urns of coarse red-burnt clay, in which were human ashes. . . . A well-formed arrow-head, two scrapers, and other tools of flint, were found in immediate proximity to the urns. The Calder-stones form a circle about six yards in diameter, and consist of six stones, five of which are still upright. They are of red sandstone, all different in size and shape."—Baines, Lanc., 1870, ii. 267. Sir J. A. Picton refers to these stones in the opening chapter of his Memorials of Liverpool; and the Wavertree residence of Sir John T. Brunner, Bart., M.P.—'Druids' Cross'—has so been designated from them. The word 'calder' is probably the A.-Sax. *galdor*, 'enchantment,' 'divination,' 'magic,' etc., occurring in such compounds as *galdor-leóth*, 'magic song'; *galdor-word*, 'magic word,' 'incantation word.' Compare also A.-Sax. *galdere* or *galdra*, 'wizard,' 'enchanter.'

As Thorpe points out, in his glossary to 'Beowulf,' the word *deór* (*dýr*) applied to a warrior does not, as in modern usage, imply reproach, any more than do the names Wulf, Biörn (bear), Hengest (stallion), Horsa (horse), etc.

Whiston.—This name is a corruption of the A.-Sax. *hwít-stán*, 'white stone.'[1] The old Whiston Hall and its outbuildings, still to be seen, are built of white stone. The same etymology applies to another Whiston—that near Rotherham—where are large quarries of white stone. The Lancashire Whiston occurs, in fact, in the Nonarum Inquisitiones (*temp.* Edw. III.), fol. 40^b, as *Whitstan*.

Widnes.—The spelling in 1285 was *Vidnes*; other later renderings have been *Wydnes* and *Wydness*. This is generally taken to be 'the wide nose (or promontory)'—O. Nor. *vídhr* (Dan. and Swed. *vid*) 'wide'; and *nös* or *nes* (Dan. *næse*, Swed. *näsa*) 'nose'; but as the Widnes promontory does not seem to be particularly wide—at any rate, at the present day—it is a moot point whether, instead of the O. Nor. *vídhr* ('wide'), the O. Nor. *vidhr* (short *i*), meaning 'a wood'—A.-Sax. *wudu*, Dan. *ved*, Swed. *väd*—was not the original component.[2]

Wigan.—The name of this town does not occur in Domesday. *Wygan* is generally the ancient appellation, and this has been referred to the A.-Sax. *wigan*, 'warriors,' 'soldiers' (sing. *wíga*; *wíg*, 'war,' 'battle'), tradition averring that in this neighbourhood, on the banks of the Douglas, King Arthur defeated the Saxons in several sanguinary encounters.[3] Whether this be so or not, the fact remains that large quantities of bones of men and horses have from time to time been turned up here.

Windle.—In Domesday, in the part relating to the land between Ribble and Mersey—" Inter Ripam et Mersham "—

---

[1] Analogy: Chaucer's *wheston* = whetstone—"A wheston is no kerving instrument."—Troil. and Cris., i. 631.

[2] Runcorn and Widnes practically form one town, but the former does not, geographically, come within the defined scope of the present monograph. It can, however, be stated that the name Runcorn occurs in the Anglo-Saxon Chronicle, under the year 913, as *Rúmcófa* (the oblique case is used, ' æt Rúmcófan ')— A.-Sax. *rúm*, 'roomy,' 'spacious'; *cófa*, 'cove,' 'creek.'

[3] See quotation from Higden's Polychronicon under DOUGLAS.

occurs a *Wibaldeslei*, which would appear to embrace the present townships of Windle, Whiston, Bold, Prescot, etc. As, however, there is no place existing in Lancashire with a name resembling *Wibaldeslei*, while there is a Wimboldsley in Cheshire, I am prepared to go further than Beamont, who thinks[1] "it is possible that the name is misplaced here [Lancashire]," and to assert that the entry of *Wibaldeslei* as being "inter Ripam et Mersham," must, beyond doubt, be a mistake on the part of a Norman scribe. As to Windle, in the Testa de Nevill we find the spellings *Wyndul* (fol. 396) and *Wyndel* (398^b). This may mean 'the pleasant dale'—A.-Sax. *wyn(n)-dæl*;[2] or the first syllable may be from a personal name. See WINSTANLEY, WINWICK.

Winstanley.—There is but one place of this name in Great Britain. It does not occur in Domesday, but in the Testa de Nevill (fol. 406) we find *Winstaneleg*; and in the Survey of 1320-1346, Chetham Soc., vol. lxxiv., 1868, we have *Wynstanleghe*. There is no etymological difficulty as to the latter portion of the name—A.-Sax. *stán*, 'stone'; *ledh*, 'lea,' 'leigh,' 'ley,' or 'meadowland' (see STANLEY); but the 'win' is a somewhat doubtful quantity. The whole name Winstanley of course simply means 'the meadowland belonging to Winstán,' which was a common enough proper name. Thus, according to Domesday, a Saxon named Winestán held our Walton in the time of the Confessor; in a charter of Æthelred's (A.D. 996)[3] we have "Wynstánes hám" (Wynstan's home); in one of Eádward's (*c*. A.D. 910),[4] "Winstánes stapol" (Winstan's pillar); a "Winstán, minister," attests one of Bishop Denewulf's charters (A.D. 879-909)[5]; and so on. But, as we have said, it is a little difficult to trace the exact meaning of *win* or *wyn* here. It certainly cannot be the A.-Sax *win*, 'wine'; it is scarcely likely to be, in this particular case, A.-Sax. *wine*, 'friend,' or even A.-Sax. *wyn* or *wynn*, 'pleasant,' 'beautiful'; and we may reject the Welsh *gwyn* (mutated to *wyn*), 'white,' 'fair' (although the first element of

---

[1] Domesday Cheshire and Lancashire, 1882, p. 75.
[2] Compare *wynn-land*, 'the pleasant land,' in the poem of the Phœnix, ascribed by Sweet and others to the Northumbrian poet Cynewulf.
[3] Codex Diplomaticus, vi. 137.   [4] *Ibid.*, v. 184.   [5] *Ibid.*, v. 163.

another Saxon name, Dunstan, is probably from the Wel. *dwn*, 'dun,' 'dark'); and also the hypothesis of a corruption of 'Woden,' as in Winsborough. It is most likely A.-Sax. *win* or *winn*, 'war.' Bosworth ('A.-Sax. Dict.,' 1838), quoting Lye ('Dict. Sax. etc.,' Manning's ed., 1772), says that from this *win* we get the proper names Alwin, 'all in war'; Baldwin, 'bold in war'; Eadwin, 'happy in war'; Godwin, 'good in war'; but it is pretty clear that *win* or *wine* as a *termination* in Saxon names is the A.-Sax. *wine*, 'friend,' 'protector'—thus Leofwine = Beloved Friend.[1] Florence of Worcester, under the year 992, records that not long after the death of the blessed Oswald, Duke Æthelwine, "friend of God," of distinguished memory, passed away.[2] As a prefix, however, *win* seems often to be the A.-Sax. *win*, *winn*, 'war.' *Winstan* would therefore literally mean 'war-stone' or 'battle-stone,' which may have denoted a monument; or it may have been an archaic term for a battle-axe, or perhaps have indicated a war-(stone) house, or castle. This literal rendering of 'battle-stone' is apparently confirmed by the occurrence of the personal name *Wigstán*, which has the same meaning; although Miss Yonge[3] (who does not give Winstán) makes all her *win* nominal prefixes represent 'friend' only.

Winwick.—An old spelling is *Wynwyc*. This is probably 'the pleasant habitation'—A.-Sax. *wyn* 'pleasant'; *wic*, 'dwelling,' 'habitation,' 'village,' etc.: *wynland*, 'the pleasant land,' 'the land of joy,' occurs in the poem of the Phœnix, attributed by Sweet and others to Cynewulf. Compare the word 'winsome.'

Woolston.—In mediæval documents the spelling is often *Wolston*, which form occurs in the Nonarum Inquisitiones, *temp.* Edw. III., fol. 40. The name must be a corruption of A.-Sax. *Wulfes-tún*—'Wulf's farmstead.'

---

[1] See Kemble's Names, Surnames, and Nic-names of the Anglo-Saxons, *Proceedings* Archæol. Inst. Gt. Britain, 1846, p. 87; and Sir J. A. Picton's Proper Names in Philological and Ethnological Enquiries, *Proceedings* Lit. and Phil. Soc. L'pool, vol. xx. (1865-66), p. 188.

[2] "Nec diu post excessum beati Oswaldi, egregiæ dux memoriæ Æthelwinus, *Dei Amicus*, defunctus est."—Florentius Wigorniensis, Thorpe's ed., 1848, i. 149.

[3] History of Christian Names, 1884.

Woolton.—This name is literally a wolf in sheep's clothing: it has nothing in common with the hair of the well-known animal any more than that of Woolwich has. Little Woolton is identified with the Domesday *Ulventune*, and Much Woolton with the Domesday *Uvetone*. Local historians have presumed from these names that the district at the time of the Saxon (or Norse) settlement was infested by wolves (A.-Sax. *wulf*, O. Nor. *úlfr*, Dan.-Norw. *ulv*, Swed. *ulf*, 'wolf'); but there is little doubt that *Ulventune* and *Uvetone* were originally the *túns* or farmsteads of a proprietor bearing the common Teutonic name Wulf or Ulf. Wolvesey, a little island near Winchester, was, however, the scene of the annual payment of the Welsh tribute of wolves' heads.

II.—HUNDRED OF WIRRAL.

Arrowe (fourteenth century, *Arwe*), like Landican, its near neighbour, may with comparative safety be deemed a relic of Celtic nomenclature—Wel. *erw*, 'acre,' 'piece of ploughland'; connected with Lat. *aro*, Gr. ἀρόω, A.-Sax. *erian*, 'to plough'; and hence Eng. 'arable.'

Backford.—The first element is Dano-Saxon for 'brook'—O. Nor. *bekkr*, Dan.-Norw. *bæk*, Swed. *bäck*, Nor. Eng. *beck*, Ger. *bach*.

Barnston.—The Domesday spelling is *Bernestone;* while in early charters the name also occurs as *Berinston*, and *Bernstone*, as well as *Barnston*, the present day rendering. It may possibly be due to a combination of a common Norse personal appellation meaning 'a bear,' *viz.*, Biörn (genit. sing. Biarnar), with the O. Nor. *steinn*, 'a stone' (monument); but it is much more probable that the place was originally the *tún* or farmstead of a Saxon settler named Beorn (genit. sing. or possess. Beornes), an appellation denoting 'one bold in war.'

Bebington.—This was a branch *tún* or settlement of the Saxon Bæbing family.[1]

Bidston.—The name of this place is found in 1272 as *Byddeston*. There is little doubt that the first element here represents the patronymic borne by the Saxon owner of the original *tún* or farmstead, although I place on record the suggestion of local archæologists that, as a runic stone has been found at Upton (about two miles from Bidston) containing the A.-Sax. verb *biddan*, 'to pray,' the name of

[1] Birch's ed. (1876) of Kemble's Saxons in England, i. 457.

the township is an attenuated form of *biddende-stán*, 'praying-stone.'

Birkenhead.—Ormerod's "head of the River Birken"[1] having been satisfactorily disposed of by local antiquaries, it is easy to fall back upon the obvious—*birken-head*, 'head or promontory of the birches'—O. Nor. *biörk*, A.-Sax. *birce*, 'birch'; O. Nor. *höfud*, A.-Sax. *heáfod*, 'head.' Hence the name Woodside. Birkenhead is not mentioned in Domesday. The earliest recorded spellings of the name are: *Birkenheved, Birkhened, Byrkehed, Birchened, Byrchened, Byrkenhed, Byrkchened, Birkynhede*, etc.

Blacon.—The Domesday spelling is *Blachehol*, which in later times seems to have been corrupted into *Blaken*. With the Norman *ch* as usual equating *k*, Blachehol clearly represents 'black hole'—A.-Sax. *blæc*, 'black,' and *hol*, 'hole,' 'hollow.' A connection with the A.-Sax. *blác* (1) 'bright, (2) 'bleak,' would scarcely be appropriate.

Brimstage.—This name occurs in early documents as *Brunstath* and *Brynstath* (and even *Brynston*), indicating that this was the stead or place—O. Nor. *stathr* (A.-Sax. *stede*)—settled by a Norseman named Brun or Bryn—O. Nor. *brúnn* (A.-Sax. *brún*, Scand. *brun*), 'brown,' 'dark.' This personal name frequently occurs in early charters. See BRYN and BROMBOROUGH.

Bromborough.—Before attempting to deal with the etymology of this name, it is necessary to consider the evidence for and against the identification of Bromborough with the Brunanburh around (*ymbe*) which Æthelstan, in A.D. 937, achieved his great victory over the allied Danes, Irish, Scots, and Welsh. The site of the battle of Brunanburh has long been a subject of controversy, but until comparatively recently the claims of Bromborough to be considered the scene of the sanguinary conflict, probably owing to the former secludedness and insignificance of the township, have scarcely been thought worth discussing. Thus Gibson merely mentioned the fact that there was a place in Cheshire called 'Brunburh,'[2] a statement which

---
[1] Chesh., 1819, ii. 254.
[2] "Oppidum est in agro Cestrensi hodie Brunburh dictum."—*Chronicon Saxonicum*, 1692.

Bosworth ('A.-Sax. Dict.,' 1838) repeats. Thorpe, in his edition of the Saxon Chronicle (1861), was unable to locate Brunanburh; so was Earle in his (1865); but Plummer, re-editing Earle's edition in 1889, queries the county of Durham, as advocated in Bosworth and Toller's 'A.-Sax. Dict.' (1882), and prefers, with Powell, to think that the battle was fought in Lancashire. Thomas Baines, however, in 'Lancashire and Cheshire, Past and Present,' 1867, i. 316, was of the opinion that it took place near Bromborough in Wirral.

Some correspondence on the subject is to be found in the *Athenæum* of the second half of 1885. In the issue of that journal for August 15, 1885, p. 207, Dr. R. F. Weymouth entertains no doubt that Bromborough in Cheshire is Brunanburh, and he speaks of "traces of a great battle in that neighbourhood." In the issue for August 22, 1885, p. 239, the Rev. T. Cann-Hughes points out that the question has been discussed in the *Cheshire Sheaf*, that Mr. John Layfield shows that on the Ordnance Survey for Bromborough parish the 'Wargreaves' is mentioned as the site of a battle between Æthelstan and the Danes in 937, and that in the *Proceedings* of the Chester Archæological Society (vol. ii.) there is a paper by the secretary, Mr. Thomas Hughes, in which it is stated that about 910 the Princess Æthelfleda built a fortress at Brimsbury, which is identified by local authorities with Bromborough. Another contributor to this correspondence, however, asserts Brunanburh to be in Dumfries-shire; another claims it to be near Axminster, while Mr. Herbert Murphy, writing in the *Athenæum* of October 3, 1885, p. 436, thinks that Mr. Hardwick, in his 'Ancient Battlefields in Lancashire' (1882), has made out an irresistible case in favour of the country round Bamber Bridge, just south of Preston and the Ribble, stress being rightly laid on the discovery, in 1840, in this locality of the famous Cuerdale collection of coins.

On the other hand, Dr. Birch, in his 'Cartularium Saxonicum' (1885, etc.), ii. viii., maintains that Brunan-burh is a poetical alliteration for *Bruninga feld*, which occurs in a Latin charter of King Æthelstan, A.D. 938 ('Cart. Sax.,' ii. 435), and, arguing that an English Broomfield or Bromfield must supply the site of the conflict, he suggests Broomfield in Somersetshire. I must confess that this portion of Dr. Birch's reasoning does not convince me. Brunnanburh or Brunan-burh *may* be a form in which historical accuracy is sacrificed to poetical demands; but the fact that a charter refers casually to the battle having been fought at or in Bruninga-feld need not count for much. This name strikes one as a generalization, meaning simply 'the plain of the Brunings,' *i.e.*, of the descendants of Brun; and, in fact, this occurrence of Bruninga-feld might seem to some to tend to the confirmation of the theory that Cheshire witnessed the battle of Brunanburh, for in this county we have, in comparative contiguity, at least three places which may owe their name to an eponymic Brun—namely, Bromborough (formerly Brunborough, Brunbræ, etc.), Brimstage (formerly Brunstath), and Brinnington. Besides, as to Bruninga-feld representing a modern Bromfield or Broomfield (Bartholomew's Gazetteer gives three Bromfields and five Broomfields in England), it must not be overlooked that a sharp labial, as *f* is, is not so liable to convert a preceding *n* into *m* as a flat labial like *b* is; and a Bromfield or Broomfield, just the same as a Bromley or Brompton, may generally be taken to imply a place which was overrun with broom.

In the map entitled 'Die Britischen Inseln bis auf Wilhelm den Eroberer, 1066,' in the Spruner-Menke 'Hand-Atlas für die Geschichte des Mittelalters' (1880), Brunanburh is placed on the 'Meresige' in about the present position of Bromborough. A gentleman who has given much study to the question on the spot, the Rev. E. D. Green, Rector of Bromborough, wrote to Mr. Helsby, the editor of Ormerod ('Hist. Chesh.,' 1882, ii. 427): "A large tract of land near the seashore at Bromborough has long been known by the name of *Wargraves*. This fact, and that of the recent discovery (June, 1877) of a large number of skeletons near the coast of the Dee, a few miles further off, with other circumstances, combine to prove that this parish was the unquestionable site of Æthelstan's famous victory over the Danes and their allies in 937."

There are one or two other points which would appear to add strength to the theory of the Battle of Brunanburh having been fought in Cheshire. In the first place it is probable—given the actual existence of a Brunanburh—that there was but one Brunanburh in England in A.D. 937, just as there is but one Bromborough to-day. Secondly, the Dee and the Mersey, whose estuaries are divided by the Wirral Peninsula, have, from time immemorial, been the favourite points of embarkation for and debarkation from Ireland; it is, indeed, tolerably certain that the first Irish missionaries to visit England landed in Wirral.[1] Thirdly, we know that a considerable Norse and Danish population had already settled in Wirral when Anlaf's ships crossed the Irish sea, and the Hiberno-Danish king could surely reckon upon the support of his fellow-countrymen.

The fact that certain land at Bromborough is known as the Wargraves is, however, of no significance. The Early English *werre*, 'war' (if that be the word intended), was not in use at the time of the battle, *wíg* being the ordinary A.-Sax. word, and the one used in the poem-chronicle[2] itself. The A.-Sax. *græf* (pl. *græfas*)—whence Mod. Eng. 'grave'—certainly meant 'trench,' 'ditch,' or 'pit'; but without evidence of early spelling it is not safe to say what the *war* in Wargraves positively represents. (Is it the A.-Sax. *waru*, 'defence,' or A.-Sax. *wær*, 'sea,' or A.-Sax. *waroth*, 'shore,' or A.-Sax. *wer*, 'fishing-place'?) Besides, the terminations *grave* and *graves* in place-names are usually attributable to A.-Sax. *gráf* (pl. *gráfas*), 'grove.' But see WARGRAVE in the West Derby Section.

The question may now be asked, Is the available evidence fairly conclusive in favour of Bromborough being Brunanburh? I am afraid that the answer must be that it is not. And for this reason, namely, that the indefatigable researches of Mr. T. T. Wilkinson[3] and Mr. Chas. Hardwick,[4] combined with the Cuerdale find of coins, leave scarcely room for doubt that the great battle of A.D. 937 was fought in the northern portion of that principal part of Lancashire

---

[1] See Helsby's ed. Ormerod's Hist. Chesh., 1882, ii. 486.
[2] The reader scarcely needs to be reminded of Tennyson's metrical version of the Battle of Brunanburh.
[3] *Transactions* Hist. Soc. Lanc. and Chesh., 1856-57, pp. 21 *sqq*.
[4] Hist. of Preston, 1857; and Ancient Battlefields in Lancashire, 1882.

which lies between Ribble and Mersey. Mr. Wilkinson makes out a very good case for the neighbourhood of Burnley, which is on the river Brun,[1] and was formerly known as Brunley, while close by are Saxifield and Danes House. Mr. Hardwick argues for the district south of Preston, and points to such names as Bamber and Brindle. A theory reconciling these two diverse views would make out that the battle was actually fought at or near Burnley, that the defeated Danes and Irish were pursued to their ships in the Ribble, and that, when that river was reached, the chest constituting the Cuerdale find had to be hurriedly buried to prevent its falling into the hands of the enemy. The Cuerdale treasure-trove, it may be recalled, consisted of (besides ingots, etc.) some 10,000 silver coins enclosed in a chest. The greater number of the coins were Danish; a large number were Anglo-Saxon, and a smaller number were French, the remainder being made up of Italian and Oriental pieces.[2] The fact that specially interests us now, however, is that *all these coins were minted between* A.D. 815 and A.D. 930, and they must consequently have been inhumed within a comparatively short period after the latter date, that is to say, about the time of the Battle of Brunanburh. Worsæ remarks,[3] with needless caution, that "the treasure must have been buried in the first half of the tenth century."

As we have therefore decided that Bromborough is not Brunanburh, it will be as well to note the early forms of the name Bromborough as they are given by Mr. Green, who writes:[4] "In 912 we have it 'Brimburgh,' and before the Conquest it is 'Brunsburg,' 'Brunnesburgh,' and 'Brimesburgh'; in 1152 'Brunborough'; *tem.* Pope Honorius, 'Brumburc'; *tem.* Edward I. (in its charter) 'Brumburgh' and 'Bromburgh'; in 1291 'Bromborch'; in 1548 'Brombrogh,' 'Brumburgh,' and 'Brumborowe'; *tem.* Eliz. 'Brumbrow'; in 1719 'Brombrough,' and since

[1] It should be noted that in the Annales Cambriæ we have "Bellum Brune," and in the Brut y Tywysogion, or Chronicle of the (Welsh) Princes, "Ac y bu ryfel Brun"—"And the Battle of Brun took place."
[2] See the *Numismatic Chronicle* (Journal of the Numismatic Soc.), 1842-43, pp. 1-120, with ten plates.
[3] Danes and Norwegians in England, 1852, p. 49.
[4] Helsby's Ormerod's Hist. Chesh., 1882, ii. 427.

'Bromborough' (pron. *Brumborough*)." The pre-Conquest forms point to the personal name Brun[1]—A.-Sax. *brún*, or O. Nor. *brúnn*, 'brown,' 'dark'—combined with A.-Sax. *burh* or *burg*, or O. Nor. *borg*, 'castle,' 'fortress';[2] and I am therefore unable to agree with Mr. Irvine's derivation of the first element of 'Bromborough,'[3] *viz.*, O. Nor. *brunnr*, 'well,' 'spring.' See BRIMSTAGE (Wirral Hundred) and BRYN (West Derby Hundred).

Burton.—This is a common English place-name, which Taylor says ('Names and their Histories,' p. 79) "is usually from the A.-Sax. *búr-tún*, which denoted a *tún* or farmyard containing a *búr* or 'bower,' the word *búr* meaning a 'storehouse' in O. Nor., and in A.-Sax. a 'chamber,' 'sleeping place,' or building of some kind"; but, as I have pointed out to Canon Taylor (who writes that he cannot affirm that my point is wrong), this explanation of the name seems lame on the face of it, for surely every farmstead, ancient or modern, must of necessity have possessed or possesses accommodation of this kind. The difficulty is got over, I think, by taking the *búr* in the *búr-túns* to represent not an apartment but a husbandman, tiller of the soil, working farmer, corresponding to the Du. *boer*, Ger. *bauer*, Platt-Deutsch *buur*, from the first of which our lexicographers, including Skeat, have derived the Eng. 'boor,' whereas 'boor' has a continuous history in England, from A.-Sax. (*ge*) *búr* onwards through Middle English, and it is found in 'neighbour,' originally 'the near farmer.' See Bosworth-Toller's 'A.-Sax. Dict.,' and Stratmann-Bradley's 'M. E. Dict.', *s.v.* The *búr* seems to have been near akin to the *ceorl*. The synonymy of mod. *boor* and *churl* apparently proves this. Taylor enumerates some 60 Burtons and 77 Carltons, Charltons, and Chorltons—not a very wide divergence.

[1] Brunswick in Germany, formerly *Brunesvic*, represents 'Bruno's habitation.'

[2] It is curious to note that, while the A.-Sax. *burg*, originally signifying an isolated stronghold (from A.-Sax. *beorgan*, 'to protect'), acquired the signification of 'city' at a very early period, the Scand. *borg* still largely tends to retain its primary meaning of 'castle,' 'fort,' 'palace.' This is, of course, due to the vastly different economic conditions which have prevailed in England and Scandinavia.

[3] *Transactions* Hist. Soc. Lanc. and Chesh., 1891-92, pp. 279 *sqq.*

In the Laws of Ine (a king of Wessex), sec. 'Be gefeohtum' (Fights), it is interesting to note how the scale of punishment fluctuates according as the brawl takes place in the king's palace, an abbey, a nobleman's or high official's residence, or the homes of the taxpayer and the *boor*.

Sir Henry Ellis points out[1] that Lord Coke calls the Bordarii of Domesday "*boors* holding a little house with some land of husbandry, bigger than a cottage"; and Sir Henry further observes:[2] "The Bures, Buri, or Burs are noticed in the first volume of Domesday as synonymous with Coliberti. . . . The name of the Coliberti was unquestionably derived from the Roman Civil Law. They are described by Lord Coke as tenants in free socage by free rent."

Caldy.—Domesday has *Calders*, which may refer to the two *Caldys*—Great and Little. Caldy is Scandinavian for 'bleak island'—O. Nor. *kald(r)* (Dan. *kold*, Swed. *kall*), 'bleak,' 'cold'; *ey*, 'island';—but as Caldy can scarcely be called an island—at any rate at the present day—this is probably an instance where O. Nor. *ey*, as is sometimes the case with A.-Sax. *ig* (= iy), represents a place beside water rather than land entirely surrounded by water.

Capenhurst occurs in Domesday as *Capeles*, which is Old French (Low Lat. *capella*) for 'chapels'; but 'Capenhurst' makes its appearance early in the fourteenth century. The 'hurst' (A.-Sax. *hyrst*, 'wood') is, seemingly, a post-Domesday suffix, and the present name, although Mr. Irvine[3] thinks it may represent "the brushwood where the capon was reared," would appear to be simply a corruption of, or false analogy for, *Capelhurst* (or *Capelshurst*), 'the wood by the chapel (or chapels).' "The township," wrote Ormerod,[4] "is judiciously broken by plantations."

Chester was the *Deva* of the Romans, from the name of

---

[1] Introduction to Domesday, 1816, xxvi.
[2] *Ibid.*, xxvii. See also Birch's ed. (1876) of Kemble's Saxons in England, i. 131, 215, 216, 225, 226; and Seebohm, English Village Community, 1884, pp. 131 *sqq*. Prof. Maitland says:—"Next above the *servi* we see the small but interesting class of *burs*."—Domesday Book and Beyond, 1897, p. 36.
[3] *Transactions* Hist. Soc. Lanc. and Chesh., 1891-92, pp. 279 *sqq*.
[4] Chesh., 1819, ii. 314.

its river (see DEE).[1] It was long the headquarters of the famous Twentieth Legion, and became known as *Castrum Legionis*, or *Castra Legionis*, 'fort' or 'camp of the legion,' and *Civitas Legionum*, 'city of the legions.' The Britons called it *Caer Lleon*—Wel. *caer*, 'fort,' 'city'; *lleon*, formed from *legione*, the ablative case of Lat. *legio*, 'legion.' The Saxons in their turn styled it *Legaceaster*, 'the legion chester' (A.-Sax. *ceaster*, 'city,' from Lat. *castra*, 'camp'). In the Saxon Chronicle, in the portion dealing with Alfred's wars with the Danes, we read (A.D. 894) that the latter "gedydon on ánre westre ceastre on Wírhealum seo is Legaceaster geháten" (arrived at a waste chester in Wirral which is called Legaceaster).[2] The prefix was eventually dropped.

Childer Thornton.—This place is not mentioned in Domesday. The name has suffered no alteration in the course of centuries. Saxon Thorntons (*túns* or farmsteads which took their name from the thorn-bush) are common enough in England, but this is the only one with the prefix *Childer*, which is the Mdle. Eng. nominative and genitive plural of *child-e* (A.-Sax. *cild*). 'Childe,' in the Middle Ages, was a title of honour borne by the sons of noblemen— as a rule until they attained the rank of knighthood. The term is familiar to readers of the present day through Byron's 'Childe Harold.' In local names it seems to have survived in Child's Wickham (Glouc.), Child's Hill (M'sex.), Child's Ercall (Salop), Childerley (Cambs.), etc. Bardsley, in his 'English Surnames' (pp. 202, 534), quotes from mediæval records such names as Ralph le Child, Walter le Child, Roger le Childe, etc. It is not probable that the above-mentioned place-names have any connection (as some have hinted) with the O. Nor. *kelda*, Dan.-Norw. *kilde*, 'well,' 'spring.'

Chorlton.—The Chorltons in England are not so numerous as the paronymous Charltons and (Nor. Eng.)

---

[1] "How Deva came to be the name of Chester or the Castra Legionis (whence the Welsh *Caer Lleon*) is not clear; possibly it was at first the camp *Ad Devam*, or 'by the Dee.'"—Rhys, Celtic Britain, 1884, p. 292.

[2] "*Civitatem Legionum*, tunc temporis desertam, quæ Saxonice *Legeceaster* dicitur ... intrant."—Florence of Worcester, A.D. 894. And "Civitas quæ *Karlegion* Britannice, et *Legeceastre* dicitur Saxonice."—*Ibid.*, A.D. 908.

Carltons—A.-Sax. *ceorl* (Eng. *churl*), Scand. *karl*, 'common man,' 'fellow.' The Carltons, Charltons, and Chorltons, like the Hintons, were originally no doubt, as a rule, the living-places allotted to the agricultural and pastoral helpers on a large estate, but it is probable that some were little *túns* or farmsteads cultivated independently by small freemen.

Claughton was formerly called *Claghton*, *Claighton*, and *Clayton*, names evidently due to the large beds of clay (A.-Sax. *clǽg*) found in the township.

Croughton or **Croghton.**—It is somewhat difficult to give with certainty the meaning of the first element of this rather uncommon Saxon place-name. Did the name, as appears most likely, signify originally 'the crook or crooked *tún*,' or rather 'the *tún* in the crook, bend, or corner'—Mdle. Eng. *crók*, *cróc*, O. Nor. *krókr* (Dan.-Norw. *krog*, Swed. *krok*), 'anything crooked,' 'nook' or 'corner'? Or did saffron (A.-Sax. *croh*) perhaps grow there? Or was crockery (A.-Sax. *croc*, *crog*, *crogh*) made there? See CROXTETH in the West Derby section. Croughton is the Domesday *Crostone*, the *s*, as in *Lestone* = Leighton, being the Norman representation of the Saxon guttural.

Dee.—It has been usual to consider that the Celtic name of this river, and of others similarly designated, represented 'dark (water)'—Wel. *dû* (dee), Gael. *dubh* (duv, doo), 'black,' 'dark' (see DOUGLAS in the West Derby section), just as the Don rivers were considered referable either to Gael. *doimhne*, 'deep,' or *donn*, 'dark brown';[1] but Professor Rhys has a more elaborate explanation. The word *Deva*, he says,[2] "originally denoted 'the river,' or rather 'the goddess of the river,' for Deva is only the feminine corresponding to a masculine *dêvo-s*, 'a god'; but when the old terminations were dropped *dêvos* and *dêva* assumed the same form, and this, according to rule, yielded in Old Welsh *doiu* or *duiu*." The modern Welsh name of the Dee is *Afon* [river] *Dyfrdwy*.

---

[1] See a paper, 'Place-names of Scotland,' by the late Prof. Blackie, in *Blackwood* for July, 1894, in which the following works are passed in review: (1) Scottish Land Names, by Sir Herbert Maxwell, 1894; (2) Place-names of Scotland, by Rev. Jas. B. Johnston, 1892; (3) Place-names of Argyllshire, by Prof. Mackinnon, in the *Scotsman*, 1888; (4) Place-names of Strathbogie, by Jas. MacDonald, 1891.

[2] Celtic Britain, 1884, p. 291.

Eastham.—The Domesday spelling of the name of Nathaniel Hawthorne's "finest old English village I have seen" is *Estham*. It has been suggested with probability that this Anglo-Saxon *hamm*,[1] or extent of land, was so named because it lay in an easterly direction from the settlement—Willaston—whence the Norman name of the Hundred of Wirral was derived.

Egremont.—This place, like its neighbour, New Brighton, is modern, and it takes its name indirectly from the ancient Cumberland Egremont, a name which originally denoted the castle built on an artificial mount by a Norman grantee soon after the Conquest. *Egremont* signifies 'the bold mount'—O. Fr. *egre* (Lat. *acer*), 'bold'; *mont*, 'mount.' Wordsworth has a poem entitled 'The Horn of Egremont Castle.' The Cumberland Egremont is referred to in a Latin charter *temp.* King John as *Acrimons*.[2]

Ellesmere.—Ellesmere Port is situated at the mouth of the canal which commences at the Ellesmere in Shropshire whence our little port borrowed its name. In 'Ellesmere' we have the same personal appellation that figures in the Derbyshire 'Alsop,' which in Domesday was written *Elleshope*. As in the case of Liverpool and Hoylake, the Salopian town has taken the name of the sheet of water upon whose shores it has risen into being.

Fender.—This is the old name of two streams in Wirral, upon the northernmore of which the Ordnance Survey, for some reason, has bestowed the new appellation of Birket. The meaning of 'Fender' here is rather obscure. Some have gone so far as to connect the latter element of the name with the Wel. *dwr*, 'water'; others observe in the former element the A.-Sax. and O. Nor. *fen*, 'mud.' Seeing, however, that the Wirral farmers seem to call any kind of large ditch or drain a fender, it is not improbable that the term is of comparatively modern origin, and was primarily used for the reason that the streams were fenders, *i.e.*, protectors, against inundations, which were formerly

---

[1] A.-Sax. *ham(m)*, 'enclosure,' is distinct from A.-Sax. *hám*, 'home,' which is generally affixed to a personal name. See Leo, Die Angelsächsischen Ortsnamen (Rectitudines Singularum Personarum), Halle, 1842, pp. 27 *sqq.*; and Kemble, Codex Diplomaticus, iii. xxvii., xxviii.

[2] Jefferson, Hist. and Antiquities of Cumberland, ii. (1842) 24.

much more prevalent in Wirral than at the present day. Sluices are sometimes called fenders in England (see the 'Hist. Eng. Dict.,' *s.v.* 'Fender').

Frankby.—This Norse name, omitted in Domesday, may well be supposed to indicate a *by* or settlement of a Frank or Franks. See a footnote under GAYTON.

Gayton.—This place occurs in Domesday as *Gaitone*. I was at first, despite the characteristic Anglo-Saxon termination of the name, inclined to think that the *tún* or settlement, like many of the contiguous townships, was of Norse foundation, and that the first element of the name was referable (1) to the O. Nor. *gata* (A.-Sax. *geat*, as in Gateshead,[1] Highgate, etc.), 'thoroughfare,' 'way,' 'road,' in allusion to the fact that Gayton is situated on the direct road, on the western or Norse side, between the northern and southern ends of the Wirral Peninsula, *i.e.*, between West Kirkby and Shotwick; or perhaps (2) to the O. Nor. *geit*[2] (A.-Sax. *gát*), 'goat,' which occasionally occurs in place-names; and, again, I judged it not impossible that the hamlet might have been founded by a *Geát* or *Gaut*(*r*), *i.e.*, Goth, from Southern Sweden, just as Frankby may owe its name to a Frankish immigrant or immigrants.[3]

[1] A curious history attaches to the name Gateshead. Bede, by what we must consider to be a remarkable error, translated *Gátesheved* by *Caput Capræ* (Goat's Head), although the classical genitive singular of A.-Sax. *gát*, 'goat,' is *gáte* or *gǽte*, not *gátes*; and the error has been perpetuated through Somner (Dict. Sax.-Lat.-Angl., 1659), Bosworth (A.-S. Dict., 1838), and even Toller (ed. Bosworth's A.-S. Dict., 1882, etc.), and Canon Taylor (Names and their Hist., 1896) down to the present day. The name is, there seems little doubt (despite the analogy of other "animal-head" names), referable to the A.-Sax. *geat*, *gæt*, or *gat* (genit. sing. *gates*), (1) 'gate,' 'door'; (2) 'street,' 'road,' 'passage,' and means 'the head or end of the road.' Mr. Richardson, Librarian to the Literary and Philosophical Society of Newcastle-on-Tyne, writes to me: "I think your explanation of the name of Gateshead is the correct one. . . . The road of which it was the head is the Roman road from Chester-le-Street, which terminated at Gateshead."

[2] O. Nor. *ei* = O. Eng. *á*, not as pronounced in Southern England, like *a* in 'father,' but as pronounced in Northern England and Scotland, *i.e.*, the Scandinavian-infected parts, like *a* in 'gate.'

[3] In Saxon poems of presumed Scandinavian or Anglian origin Swedes and Goths, and also Franks and Frisians, are mentioned together in a similar manner to the Picts and Scots. Thus in "that

On the whole, however, it would appear that Gayton was merely a Saxon goat-farm. We have the analogy of Gatton, in Surrey, which is mentioned in the Will of Duke Ælfred (A.D. 871-889)[1] as *Gatatun*—A.-Sax. *gáta*, genit. pl. of *gát*, 'goat.' A *gáta-hús* was a goat-house.

Gowy.—The name of the river at the southern end of the Wirral peninsula is clearly connected with the Welsh *gwy*, 'water.'[2]

Greasby.—This Norse-looking name seems really to be of Saxon origin, for it occurs in Domesday as *Gravesberie*. The A.-Sax. *græf*[3] (O. Nor. *gröf*), the genitive singular of which is *græfes*, meant (1) 'trench,' 'ditch'; (2) 'grave'; while A.-Sax. *gráf* (genit. sing. *gráfes*) signified 'grove.' Gravesberie, and therefore Greasby, must, however, simply be the A.-Sax. *Græfes-burh*, 'the castle of Græf.' Such patronymics as Graves, Groves, and Trench are common enough to-day.

Hargrave.—Domesday has *Haregrave*. The name might seem to indicate that considerable earthworks were here thrown up by the usurping Scandinavians. The O. Nor. *her-gröf* (Dan. *hær-grav*, Swed. *här-graf*) may be construed as 'military trench'; other similar O. Nor. compounds include *her-floti*, 'war-fleet'; *her-fólk*, 'war-people'; *her-klædhi*, 'war-clothing,' *i.e.*, 'armour,' the O. Nor. *herr* (A.-Sax. *here*, Ger. *heer*) primarily signifying 'host,' 'army.' As to the easy phonetic interchange of *her* and *har* compare the various Hardwicks (cattle stations) in England, the first element of the name usually being the A.-Sax. *heord*, 'herd'; and Hertford = Hartford or Harford, Derby = Darby, Berk-

---

ancient and curious nomenclature of persons and places," The Scôp or Gleeman's Tale, we read "mid Sweóm and mid Geátum "—with the Swedes and Goths; while in Beowulf occurs "under Froncum and Frysum"—among the Franks and Frisians; and in The Scôp or Gleeman's Tale, again, "mid Froncum . . . and mid Frysum"—with the Franks and Frisians.

[1] Kemble, Codex Diplomaticus, ii. 120; Thorpe, Diplomatarium Anglicum, p. 480; Birch, Cartularium Saxonicum, ii. 195.

[2] Prof. Kuno Meyer (The Voyage of Bran: an Old Irish Saga, 1896-7, i. 38) says that perhaps the obscure Ir. *fía* is cognate with Wel. *gwy*, and means 'water.'

[3] At the end of syllables and between two vowels A.-Sax. $f = v$.

shire = Barkshire, etc.[1] Again, the prefix *har* in place-names in Danish-settled parts of England may sometimes be the O. Nor. *hár*,[2] 'high'; and perhaps O. Nor. *harr* (A.-Sax. *hár*), 'hoary,' 'grey.' (See GREASBY.) But in the case of Hargrave we think we must agree with Canon Bardsley,[3] that it represents simply 'the hare grove'—A.-Sax. *hara*, Scand. *hare*, 'hare'; A.-Sax. *gráf*, 'grove'—just as Congreve means 'the coney (rabbit) grove.'

Heswall.—The name of this township occurs in Domesday as *Eswelle;* but in the thirteenth century we have *Haselwell*, and Ormerod, in 1819, calls it *Haselwall*. The name doubtless originally signified 'the field or plain of the hazels'—O. Nor. *hasl*, 'hazel,' *plus* the usual O. Nor. *völlr* (dat. sing. *velli*), 'field.'

Hilbre (Island).—It is really superfluous to add 'Island' after Hilbre, which contains the old word for 'island' in itself. The ancient name was *Hildburgheye, i.e.,* 'the isle of Hildburgha'—O. Nor. *ey*, 'island.'[4]

Hoose.—The name of this little extra-parochial township is derived from the plural of A.-Sax. *hó* (hoo) = 'hough' or 'heel' (of land). See HOOTON.

Hooton.—Domesday spelling, *Hotone*, 'the *tún* or farmstead on the hough or heel of land'—A.-Sax. *hó*, 'heel,' 'hough.' Kemble says:[5] "Originally a point of land, formed like a heel, or boot, and stretching into the plain; perhaps even into the sea."

Hoylake.—The name of this favourite golfing resort has this much in common with that of Liverpool— in both

---

[1] William Mitford, in his Harmony in Language, published in 1804, says (p. 24): "A fashion has been growing to pronounce the word *merchant* (formerly written as spoken, *marchant*, from the French *marchand*) as if it were written *murchant*. Here, as in some other instances, the corruption of orthography has tended to the corruption of pronunciation."

[2] O. Nor. *á* is really a diphthong representing *a + u*, pron. *ou* or *ow*.

[3] English Surnames, 5th ed., 1897, p. 120.

[4] As an instance of what can be done in quite modern times in the way of wilfully corrupting land-names, it may be mentioned that in Bacon's Geological Map of England and Wales (1891) this island is called *Elborough* !

[5] Codex Diplomaticus, iii. xxxi.

cases the appellation of a piece of water has eventually been bestowed upon a village on its banks. As to the Hoyle Lake, Ormerod says :[1] "The adjacent lake, anciently called 'Lacus de Hilburgheye,' and 'Heye-pol' . . . derives its present name from two large sandbanks, which afford in stormy weather a salutary refuge to the vessels frequenting the port of Liverpool . . . the blending of the two lights [Bidston and Leasowe] being the signal that the vessel is right for Hoyle Lake." Having in view the Leasowe submarine forest, a wandering philologist might be tempted to assert that 'Hoyle' is the Gael. *coill* or *choill* (pron. *hoyle*), 'a wood'; but it is no doubt simply the Nor. Eng. *hoyle* = 'hole,' 'hollow' (in this case a hollow filled with water), 'lake' being added to the name when the signification of *hoyle* had been forgotten. In the South Lancashire dialect "long *o* becomes sometimes *ow*—*now* for *no;* sometimes *oy*—*hoyle* for *hole*."[2] Nodal and Milner,[3] and also Holland,[4] have *howle* but not *hoyle* in their respective glossaries; but there is no question of the former, if not of the present, existence of the form *hoyle*.

Irby.—"Hugh Lupus granted this township as 'the manor of *Erby* in Wirhalle,' in his charter to the Abbey of St. Werburgh in 1093."[5] The name of this Norse *býr* or settlement is apparently eponymous. Says Taylor :[6] "From the common Scandinavian name of Ivar or Ingvar we have Jurby in the Isle of Man, formerly Ivorby, Irby in Lincolnshire and in Yorkshire."

Landican.—Domesday spelling, *Landechene*. As the existence of a very ancient church is traced here, Mr. Irvine[7] had no difficulty in taking the first element of the name to be the common Welsh ecclesiastical *llan*, and, following a usual canon, the latter half to be the patronymic of a saint, in this case that of a holy person long forgotten. But I think we have here, instead of the Welsh *llan*, its

---

[1] Chesh., 1819, ii. 273.
[2] Picton, South Lancashire Dialect, *Proceedings* Lit. and Phil. Soc. L'pool, vol. xix. (1864-65), p. 47.
[3] Lancashire Glossary, Eng. Dial. Soc., 1875-82.
[4] Cheshire Glossary, Eng. Dial. Soc., 1884-86.
[5] Ormerod, Chesh., 1819, ii. 280.
[6] Names and their Histories, 1896, p. 351.
[7] *Transactions* Hist. Soc. Lanc. and Chesh., 1891-92, pp. 279 *sqq*.

Gaelic equivalent *lann*, whose plural is *lanndaichean*, which might explain the whole word. 'Landican' may have had the primary meaning of 'the enclosures,' or the later signification of 'the churches.'

Larton.—The old spelling was *Lareton*, which apparently means 'the marsh hamlet'—Mdle. Eng. *lar, laire,* 'marsh,' 'bog,' 'mire,' from O. Nor. *leir* (Dan., Norw., Swed., *ler*). Halliwell's 'Dict. of Archaic and Provincial Words' (1850) has *lare*, 'quagmire,' 'bog.' There are or were various *cars* or mosses in the vicinity of Larton.

Leasowes, The.—'The Pastures'—A.-Sax. *læswe*, 'a pasture.'

Ledsham is clearly eponymous. In Domesday we have *Levetesham*; and as the names of owners of neighbouring manors occur Leuvede and Leviett. The place was therefore the *hám*, or home, of this Saxon family.

Leighton.—Domesday, *Lestone*. The numerous Leightons and Leytons in England were *túns* or farmsteads on meadow or pasture land—A.-Sax. *leáh*, 'meadow,' 'pasture,' 'lea.' The *s* in the Norman *Lestone* represents the Saxon guttural; *cf. Crostone* = Croughton.

Liscard.—The meaning of this name is involved in some obscurity. Ormerod said[1] that the place was formerly called *Listark*; but this was an error for *Liscark*.[2] Irvine remarks[3] that the mediæval appellations correspond to those of Liskeard in Cornwall, with which place it is natural to compare our Liscard; and as to the Cornish town I have the following note from a respected local antiquary:

"The ancient name of Liskeard is *Lyscerruyt*, and appears so in the Bodmin Manumission Book, written, it is supposed, between A.D. 940 and 1040. It is said to be the only original record relating to Liskeard anterior to the Norman Conquest which is now extant. Liskeard was for many centuries called 'Liskerrett,' otherwise 'Liskeard.' The etymology is very uncertain, but the generally received opinion is that it is derived from *Llys* or *Lis*, 'a manor house or fort,' and *Caer*, 'a walled town.'"

---
[1] Chesh., 1819, ii. 264.
[2] Helsby's Ormerod's Chesh., 1882, ii. 478.
[3] *Transactions* Hist. Soc. Lanc. and Chesh., 1891-92, pp. 279 *sqq.*

The latter part of this derivation must at once be discarded. *Lis* is perhaps the Cymric *llj's*, 'palace,' 'hall,' 'court,' and the succeeding portion of the name may easily be the patronymic of the ancient proprietor of the estate; but I am rather inclined (at any rate as to our Cheshire Liscard) to favour a derivation from the Gael. *lis* or *lios*, 'enclosure,' etc., combined with Gael. *ceard* (the Scottish surname Caird), 'smith,' which would give 'the smith's place,' corresponding to the English Smethwicks. This etymology would appear to be clinched by a reference to Joyce.[1] He gives Liscartan as representing 'the fort [? place] of the forge,' from *ceardcha* (pron. *cardha*), 'a forge' —modern spelling *carte, cart, cartan*, etc. ; *ceard* (pron. *card*) 'smith,' 'artificer.'

Meols.—Domesday *Melas*—O. Nor. *melr* (genit. case, *mels*) 'sandhill,' 'sandbank.'

Mollington occurs in Domesday as *Molintone*. The English Mollingtons denote estates originally held by the Saxon Molling tribe or family.

Moreton indicated 'the *tún* or farmstead on or by the moor'—A. Sax. *mór*, ' moor.'

Ness, Neston.—The Domesday *Nesse* and *Nestone*. Neston was 'the *tún* or farmstead on the ness,' *i.e.*, headland—A.-Sax. *næss*, O. Nor. *nes*, ' headland,' ' promontory.'

Netherpool.—'The Lower Pool'—A.-Sax. *neother*, 'lower.'

New Brighton.—This is a modern name bestowed in imitation of the Sussex watering-place, which was anciently called *Brihthelmestan, i.e.,* 'the Stone of Brihthelm.' The A.-Sax. *stán*, literally 'stone,' 'rock,' sometimes indicated a residence or castle built of stone, or on a rock,[2] and a monumental or boundary stone. A very slight corruption of the old name of the Sussex Brighton was current up to the early years of the present century.

[1] Irish Local Names Explained, 1884, pp. 66 and 98.
[2] The Dutch and Flemish *steen* (pron. *stān*), literally 'stone,' also denotes 'a castle': the old Scheldt-side keep at Antwerp, now converted into a " Musæum van Oudheden " (Museum of Antiquities), is still called " Het Steen "—The Stone (Castle).

Noctorum.—This name has nothing to do with the Latin language, despite its genitive plural appearance. Domesday has *Chenoterie*, which, if as usual we turn the Norman *ch* back into *k*, does not bear so very distant a resemblance to the name of the township as it was spelled in the thirteenth century, *viz.*, *Knocttyrum*, or even as Ormerod (1819) has it, *Knoctorum*. The first element of these renderings at once suggests the Gael. *cnoc* (knock), 'hill.' For the second portion of the name the Gael. *druim*, 'ridge,' has been hazarded; but this is obviously impossible. We must rather, I think, look for some such word as Gael. *torran* (diminutive of *torr*), 'grave,' 'tomb.' The nearest approach to the name which I can find in Joyce's works on Irish topographic etymology is Knockatarry (Ir. *Cnoc-a'-tairbh*), 'the hill of the bull.'[1]

Overchurch is 'the church on the banks,' *i.e.*, of a mere which is now drained—A.-Sax. *ófer* ($f = v$), 'shore,' 'banks.'

Overpool.—'The Upper Pool'—A.-Sax. *ofer* ($f = v$), 'upper.' This is the Domesday *Pol*.

Oxton.—The name of this place figures in mediæval documents as *Oxon*, which some have erroneously thought to be a corruption of a British designation. There is, however, no reason why a patient animal, anciently more used than to-day, should not give its name to an Anglo-Saxon *tún* or settlement just as it has given it to a ford (Oxford) and to a creek (Oxwich). On the other hand, the name may be, and doubtless is, eponymic; we know that Oxmantown, Dublin, was originally 'Ostmentown,' or the dwelling-place of the Eastern men or Danes. It has been thought that the *Oggodestún* mentioned in the will of Wulfric Spott, Earl of Mercia, which was drawn up about 1004 A.D., referred to the Wirral Oxton; but I can see no reason to dissent from Dugdale's identification of this Oggodestún with Ogston in Derbyshire.[2] The *Ox* in 'Oxton' is, however, probably a corruption of a similar personal name in its genitive or possessive case.

---

[1] Irish Local Names Explained, 1884, p. 60.
[2] Monasticon Anglicanum, 1682, i. 266.

Parkgate.—"The name Parkgate is said to have been given by the labourers who were engaged in making the sea-wall, and its proximity to Leighton Park originated it; before that it was called New Quay or New Haven."[1]

Pensby.—In the time of Henry VI. we have *Pennesby*. The name no doubt embodies the patronymic of the founder of this Norse *by* or settlement. In Scandinavian *pen* is the equivalent of 'smart,' 'spruce,' 'nice.'

Poolton (Wallasey).
Poulton Lancelyn. }—The name of the Wallasey Poolton, not mentioned in Domesday, was formerly written *Pulton* and *Poulton*, *i.e.* 'the *tún* or farmstead by the [Wallasey] Pool'—A.-Sax. *pól*. The second Poulton, called in Domesday *Pontone* [?], took its name from the Bromborough Pool, the distinguishing suffix Lancelyn being the patronymic of ancient owners of the manor.

Prenton.—In Domesday the name of this township figures as *Prestune*. The numerous Prestons in England indicate the *túns* or habitations of priests—A.-Sax. *preóst*, 'priest.' 'Prenton' is synonymous with 'Preston.' "Eádberht, the last true-born King of Kent, was surnamed Pren, or the Priest, for he had been ordained."[2]

Puddington.—The name of this village, near the Dee, has nothing to do with Christmas cheer. In Domesday it occurs as *Potintone*. The English Puddingtons are usually considered to be settlements of the Saxon Pæting tribe. In Anglo-Saxon *t* and *d* were often used indiscriminately for each other.

Raby.—The Domesday spelling is *Rabie*. The Lancashire 'Roby' was originally identical with this name. In both 'Raby' and 'Roby' we probably have embodied the common animal-name of the earliest Scandinavian owner of the *by* or settlement, the O. Nor. *rá*, pron. as *row* = noise—Dan.-Norw. *raa*, Swed. *rå*, both pron. *raw*—meaning 'a roe.'

---

[1] Mrs. Gamlin, 'Twixt Mersey and Dee, 1897, p. 251.
[2] Kemble, Names, Surnames, and Nic-names of the Anglo-Saxons, *Proceedings* Archæol. Inst. Gt. Britain, 1846, p. 93.

Saughall.
Soughall. }—Domesday has a *Salhale*, which developed later into *Salghall*. This has (perhaps naturally) been construed as 'the hall of the sallows or willows'—A.-Sax. *sealh*, Scot. *saugh*, 'a sallow,' 'a willow;' but the A.-Sax. *healh* is sometimes a word of doubtful meaning. Kemble decided that it must represent 'a stone house,' 'a hall,' and this canon was long followed. Recent investigations, however, show that the word will very often not bear this interpretation, and that it rather means 'a slope,' which is in accordance with the signification of the O. Nor. *hall(r)*, 'a slope,' 'a hill.'[1] On the whole, therefore, we must take Saughall and Soughall to represent 'willow-slope.'

Seacombe.—The Saxons transformed the Wel. *cwm*, 'valley,' 'dale,' 'glen,' 'dingle,' into *combe*. Seacombe is close to the point where the Mersey discharges itself into the Irish Sea.

Shotwick.—Both components of this name are of somewhat uncertain origin. The Domesday spelling was *Sotowiche*, and in the thirteenth century we find *Schotewycke*, which shows that the early pronunciation was practically as it is to-day. The three best-known English place-names with the element *shot*—Aldershot, Bagshot, and Oakshot—being situated on or near the sites of ancient forests, are generally presumed to derive their last syllable from a combination of the genitive or possessive *s* with the O. Eng. *holt*, 'copse,' 'wood'; but other names with *shot*, and which have the termination *sete* in Domesday, are thought by some to be referable, as to this, to a doubtful O. Eng. *scôtu*, 'common,' 'pasture'; while Shottery (near Stratford-on-Avon), anciently *Scotta-rith*, it is concluded, might be 'trout-beck'—A.-Sax. *sceót* or *sceóta*, 'trout.'[2]

---

[1] In a description of the district (Hales Owen) where Shenstone resided, which is prefixed to an edition of the poet's works published in 1793, it is curious to note how often the word 'slope' and its derivatives are used by the writer, who probably had not the faintest idea that the name Hales was itself significative of the nature of the landscape. Sheriff Hales, also in Shropshire, is called in Domesday *Halas*, the plural of *healh*, 'a slope,' *h* after a consonant being dropped in the inflection of Anglo-Saxon nouns.

[2] See Taylor, Names and their Histories, 1896, pp. 381 and 385

Referring to Shotwick, Ormerod says[1]: "Here, as in most cases in Cheshire where this termination of name occurs, were formerly saltworks." This being so, and salt deposits having been worked at a very early period in Britain, and elsewhere — possibly in Britain by the pre-Celtic agglutinative-language (neolithic) race or races—it is not improbable that Shotwick was a Saxon ante-Norse settlement, and that the *wíc(h)* (usually meaning, 'dwelling,' 'habitation,' 'village,' 'station') of the Saxons was converted by the Vikings, *i.e.*, the Creekers, into their characteristic word for 'creek,' 'bay,' namely, *vík* (wick). We seem, however, to have fairly distinct evidence that the A.-Sax. *wíc*, besides its general signification of 'habitation' (Lat. *vicus* (1) 'quarter or street of a town,' (2) 'village,' 'hamlet'; Gr. οἶκος — pron. *weekos* — 'dwelling-place'), also meant 'a marsh.' This was Dr. Leo's supposition, and Kemble, referring to it, says[2]: "Some plausibility is given to the suggestion, partly by the frequent use of the termination *-wich* in places near salt-pools, and by the occurrence of such names as *hreódwíc* [Reedwich]." It has been thought, again, not inconceivable that Shotwick may be a corruption of *Scalt-wíc* or *Salt-wíc*. A place of this name is mentioned in a charter of Æthelbald of Mercia, A.D. 716-717,[3] and elsewhere, but it is identified with Droitwich.[4]

But, on the whole, the most probable explanation of 'Shotwick' is that which defines it as 'the (salt) station on the shot or spit of land' (perhaps extending into the river Dee)—A.-Sax. *sceát* or *sceót*, 'corner,' 'division,' 'portion,' 'tract.' In Wright's 'Dict. of Obsolete and Provincial English' (1857) *shot* = 'an angle of land,' and Halliwell's 'Dict. of Archaic and Provincial Words' (1850) has *shott* = 'field,' 'plot of land.' 'Shot' is apparently a doublet of 'sheet,' both being ultimately from A.-Sax. *sceótan*, 'to shoot,' 'to extend'; but while 'sheet' takes its pronuncia-

---

[1] Chesh., 1819, ii. 309.
[2] Codex Diplomaticus, iii. xli.   [3] *Ibid.*, i. 81.
[4] Had this theory been tenable it would have been necessary to explain that the voicing of *s* as *sh* in Old English is sporadic; 'she' is the A.-S. *seó*. In Gaelic *s*, in certain defined positions, including when preceded or followed by *e* or *i*, takes the sound over which the Ephraimites came to grief; while in Hungarian *s* has the *sh* sound pure and simple.

tion from what the author of the 'History of English Sounds' (Sweet) would call the second gradatory place in the *eó* line, *i.e.*, from the preterite singular (*sceát*), 'shot' has taken the vowel-sound of the third place, *i.e.*, from the past participle (*scoten*). Analogous words in the Teutonic languages are: Ger. *schote*, Dan.-Norw. *skjød*, Swed. *skot*, all = 'sheet' (*naut.*), while Du. *schot* is 'a partition,' 'a division.' The place-component *shot* has frequently given rise to discussion in *Notes and Queries*, the most useful references probably being 6th ser. viii. 369, 412, 523 (1883); 8th ser. i. 148, 214, 337, 419, 484 (1892). See footnote under FAZAKERLEY, in the West Derby Section.

Spital.—This is the same word with *hospital*, an Old French term, meaning 'guest-house,' which came through Low Latin from the classic *hospitium*, 'hospitality,' and, by metonymy, 'guest-chamber,' 'inn.' In Middle English *hospital* suffered apheresis and became *spital* or *spitel*. The present signification of 'hospital' is of comparatively late origin.

Stanney figured in Domesday as *Stanei*, *i.e.*, 'the stony or rocky island' (or riparian tract)—A.-Sax. *stán*, 'stone,' 'rock'; *ig* (= iy), 'island,' 'low riparian land.'

Stoke.—Our Stokes and Stocktons seem to have been generally *stock*aded places—A.-Sax. *stocc*, 'stump,' 'stake.' Occasionally, however, the name might refer (especially in marshy districts) to an erection on stakes or piles. The Stokes appear in some respects to compare with our Peels or old family fortresses or keeps[1]—A.-Sax. *píl* (Lat. *pila*), 'pile,' 'pillar.'[2]

Storeton. As this name appears as early as Domesday —as *Stortone*—it is not possible that, as has been suggested, we have here the Mdle. Eng. *stór*, meaning 'store,' 'farm-stock,' from O. Fr. *estoire*. The name doubtless signifies 'the great *tún* or farmstead'—A.-Sax. *stór* (Scand. *stór*[3]), Mdle. Eng. *stór* and *store*, 'great,' 'large,' 'strong,' a word

---

[1] "God save the lady of this *pel*."—Chaucer, Hous of Fame, iii. 220.
[2] Skeat, however, in his Glossarial Index to Chaucer, 1894, has "*pel* = peel, small castle—O. Fr. *pel*, from Lat. acc. *pálum*."
[3] We meet with the expression *stór-thorp* (n. pl.), 'large villages,' in the Saga known as the Fagrskinna.

HUNDRED OF WIRRAL

which has not come down to our day in England[1] unless it still be used in a few remote provincial districts, while it flourishes vigorously in Scandinavia.

Sutton.—Domesday *Sudtone*, 'the south *tún* or farmstead '—A.-Sax. *súth*, 'south.'

Thingwall.—Domesday has *Tinguelle*. This place was the 'Parliament Field' of the Wirral Norsemen—O. Nor. *thing*, 'parliament,' *völlr* (dat. sing. *velli*), 'field.' See THINGWALL in the West Derby Section.

Thornton Hough.—Domesday has *Torintone*; later we have *Thorneton-en-le-Hogh*. The English Thorntons (A.-Sax. *þorn*, 'thorn'; *tún*, 'farmstead') belong to the numerous class of place-names derived from large plant-life, such as Acton (Oakton), Ashton, Appleton, etc. A hogh or hough (A.-Sax. *hóh, hó*) is a point of land formed like a heel. See HOOTON.

Thurstaston.—The Domesday spelling of this Dano-Saxon name is *Turstanetone*, which early in the fourteenth century had become *Thurstaneston*. There are two possibilities here: the village may originally have been 'the *tún* (or farmstead) of Thor's stone'; or the settlement may have been named after a proprietor who boasted the same patronymic as the Norse king Thorstein, who died 874 A.D. The former theory is apparently, however, confirmed by the existence on Thurstaston Common of a large and remarkable stone or rock, which Picton[2] concluded to be a relic of Saxon or Danish heathendom.

Tranmere does not figure in Domesday. The earliest spellings recorded dispose of any apparent connection with a mere or marsh. In documents of the thirteenth century occur *Tranmull*, *Tranmoll*, and *Tranmoel*; later still we have *Tranmore*. There does not seem to be any reason to doubt the general accuracy of the etymology put forward by Mr. Irvine[3]—Wel. *Tre-yn-moel*, 'the hill settlement,' especially as this is borne out physiographically.

---

[1] Vigfusson, however, thinks it is embodied in 'sturdy,' Nor. Eng. 'stordy.'
[2] Helsby's Ormerod's Chesh., 1882, ii. 511.
[3] *Transactions* Hist. Sec. Lanc. and Chesh., 1891-92, pp. 279 *sqq*.

Upton.—This name occurs in Domesday as *Optone*, and is evidently due to the elevated situation of the Anglo-Saxon *tún* or farmstead.

Wallasey.—"The angles of the termination of the promontory of Wirral consist of two rocky elevations which have apparently been separated from the mainland by the streams of the Dee and the Mersey at some distant period. One of these is called *Walea* in Domesday, and the other *Cerchebia*, or Kirkby, in a charter of 1081. The latter of these was afterwards denominated 'West Kirkby,' as a distinction from Kirkby-in-Walley, the name assumed by the former parish as early as the thirteenth century, and which was shortly afterwards changed to *Walayesegh*."[1]

At any rate, Wallasey at the present day is almost an island, hemmed in as it is by Liverpool Bay, the Mersey, Wallasey Pool, and the Birket or Fender. Many local antiquaries have definitively accepted as the etymology of the name Wallasey the A.-Sax. combination *Weal(h)as-ig*, 'the Welshmen's island,' as it is known that the ancient Britons held their ground in the Wirral peninsula until a comparatively late period compared with other Anglo-Saxon and Scandinavian districts; but it appears to have escaped observation that upon the coast of Essex, whence the Britons were early driven, there is an island with practically the same name, *viz.*, Wallasea, which Taylor[2] says is "an island surrounded by a sea-*wall* or embankment." This is, I think, the best explanation of the name. The A.-Sax *weall* or *wall* (genit. *wealles* or *walles*; nom. pl. *weallas* or *wallas*), 'wall,' 'rampart,' etc.; the Dan.-Norw. *val*, 'bank,' 'shore'; and the Swed. and Ger. *wall*, Du. *wal*, 'dam,' 'dike,' 'rampart,' 'shore,' are from the Lat. *vallum*, 'rampart.' The suffix *ey* is the A.-Sax. *íg* (= *iy*), O. Nor. *ey*, of which *eâ*, in the case of island-names, is a corruption. We may take it that the first two syllables in 'Wallasey' and 'Wallasea' are the plural of *wall*, and not the genitive singular, and that therefore the names should be read literally as 'embankments island,' not 'embankment island,' there probably having been a series of sea-resisting dams on each island, although,

---

[1] Ormerod's Chesh., 1819, ii. 261.
[2] Names and their Histories, 1896, p. 373.

as to the Wirral island, this was apparently not the case at the time of the Domesday Survey, which, as we have seen, gives *Walea*. It is interesting to note that there exists at the present day a Wallasey Embankment Commission, whose members are elected triennially.

West Kirkby.—See under WALLASEY. In a charter of 1081 the name of this rising watering-place occurs as *Cerchebi* and *Cerchebia*, the Normanized form of the original Norse name—O. Nor. *kirkja* (Dan.-Norw. *kirke*, Swed. *kyrka*, Scot. *kirk*), 'church'; Scand. *by*, 'village.' 'West' was prefixed to 'Kirkby' in order to distinguish this church-village from the old Wallasey Kirkby.

Whitby.—The name of this village near Ellesmere Port is the Norse equivalent of the English *Whitton*, or 'white town'—O. Nor. and A.-Sax. *hwit*, 'white,' 'bright'; Scand. *by*, 'settlement,' 'village.' The Saxons and Scandinavians appear to have used the adjective *hwit*, 'white,' to distinguish stone buildings from the usual sombre wooden erections. Compare 'Whitchurch.'

Willaston.—" From circumstances which it would be vain to inquire into, the township from which the Hundred of Wirral derives its Norman name of *Wilaveston* has escaped notice in the Domesday Survey. It appears first . . . in 1230 . . . [as] *Willaston*."[1] This name without doubt embodies the personal appellation (perhaps *Wigláf*, 'War Heritage') of the original Saxon proprietor of the *tún* or manor.

Wirral.—The name of the celebrated peninsula occurs in the Anglo-Saxon Chronicle[2] as *Wirheal*, literally (probably) 'myrtle-corner'—A.-Sax. *wir*, 'a myrtle-tree'; *heal*, 'angle,' 'corner,' 'slope'; the supposition being that this corner of land was originally overgrown with bog-myrtle. It is interesting to note that one of the mediæval spellings of the name of the peninsula recurs so late as 1820 in a Crown deed conveying the bailiwick of *Wirehall* to one John Williams of Liverpool, to whom the Government sold it in fee. Mr. Mortimer has printed the conveyance *verbatim*.[3]

---

[1] Ormerod's Chesh., 1819, ii. 300.
[2] Under the year 895—Alfred's Wars with the Danes.
[3] Hist. of Wirral, 1847, p. 154.

The form *Wirhal* (" on Wirhalum ") is found in the will of Wulfric Spott (*ob.* 1010), as printed by Dugdale.[1] Sir Peter Leycester has the present spelling *Wirral* in the seventeenth century.[2]

[1] Monasticon Anglicanum, 1682, i. 266.
[2] Antiquities of Cheshire, 1673, p. 92.

LIST OF WORKS QUOTED.

[*This list does not represent all the works and records consulted: it contains only those to which actual reference is made, and it does not include dictionaries and periodicals.*]

Ancient Battlefields in Lancashire. Hardwick, 1882.
Angelsächsische Ortsnamen ('Rectitudines Singularum Personarum'). Leo, 1842.
Anglo-Saxon and Old English Vocabularies. Wright, Wülcker, 1884.
Anglo-Saxon Chronicle. Gibson's ed., 1692.
    do. Thorpe's ed., 1861.
    do. Earle's ed., 1865.
    do. Plummer's ed., 1889.
Anglo-Saxon Reader. Sweet, 1894.
Annales Cambriæ ('Monumenta Historica Britannica'). Petrie, Sharpe, Hardy, 1848.
Antiquities of Cheshire. Leycester, 1673.
Beowulf. Thorpe's 3rd ed., 1889.
Britannia. Camden, 1586 and 1607 eds.
    do.   do. Gibson's ed., 1772.
    do.   do. Gough's ed., 1789.
Brut y Tywysogion, or *Chronicle of the [Welsh] Princes* ('Monumenta Historica Britannica'). Petrie, Sharpe, Hardy, 1848.
Cartularium Saxonicum. Birch, 1885, etc.
Celtic Britain. Rhys, 1884.
Chancery Rolls (Rotuli Cancellarii).
Charter Rolls (Rotuli Chartarum).
Chaucer's Works. Skeat's ed., 1894, etc.
Cheshire Glossary. Holland. English Dialect Society, 1884-86.
Close Rolls (Rotuli Litterarum Clausarum).
Codex Diplomaticus Ævi Saxonici. Kemble. English Historical Society, 1839-48.
Corpus Poeticum Boreale. Vigfusson, Powell, 1883.
Danes and Norwegians in England. Worsæ, 1852.
Diplomatarium Anglicum Ævi Saxonici. Thorpe, 1865.
Domesday. Ellis, 1816.
Domesday Book and Beyond. Maitland, 1897.
Domesday Cheshire and Lancashire. Beamont, 1882.
Domesday Facsimile of Cheshire and Lancashire. James, 1861-63.

Duchy Records (Ducatus Lancastriæ).
English Surnames: Their Sources and Significations. Bardsley 5th ed., 1897.
English Village Community. Seebohm, 1884.
Ethelwerd's Chronicle ('Rerum Anglicarum Scriptores post Bedam'). Savile, 1601.
    do.   ('Monumenta Historica Britannica'). Petrie, Sharpe, Hardy, 1848.
Feudal England. Round, 1895.
Florence of Worcester (Florentius Wigorniensis). Thorpe's ed., English Historical Society, 1848-49.
Geographic Etymology: Dictionary of Place-Names. C. Blackie, 1887.
Glossarium Antiquitatum Britannicarum. Baxter, 1733.
Great de Lacy Inquisition, 1311 ('Three Lancashire Documents'). Chetham Society, 1868.
Greek and Latin Etymology. Peile, 1869.
Hand-Atlas für die Geschichte des Mittelalters. Spruner, Menke, 1880.
Harmony in Language. Mitford, 1804.
Historia Ecclesiastica Gentis Anglorum. Bede. Stevenson's ed., 1841.
    do.   *do.*   Plummer's ed., 1896.
Historical English Grammar. Morris, 1875.
History of Cheshire. Ormerod, 1819.
    do.   *do.* Helsby's ed., 1882.
History of Christian Names. Miss Yonge, 1884.
History of Cumberland. Jefferson, 1842.
History of English Sounds from the Earliest Period. Sweet, 1888.
History of Everton. Syers, 1830.
History of Lancashire. Baines, 1836.
    do.   *do.* Harland and Herford's ed., 1868-70.
    do.   *do.* Croston's ed., 1888-93.
History of Leverpool. Enfield, 1774.
History of Liverpool. Troughton, 1810.
    do. T. Baines, 1852.
History of Manchester. Whitaker, 1775.
History of Preston. Hardwick, 1857.
History of Sankey. Beamont, 1889.
History of Wirral. Mortimer, 1847.
Holinshed's Chronicles. Hooker's ed., 1587.
Icelandic Sagas, etc., relating to the Settlements and Descents of the Northmen on the British Isles. Vigfusson's Text, 1887; Dasent's Translation, 1894.
Irish Local Names Explained. Joyce, 1884.
Irish Names of Places. 2nd ser. Joyce, 1875.
Itinerary (Leland). Hearne's 2nd ed., 1744.
Lancashire and Cheshire, Past and Present. T. Baines, 1867.
Lancashire and Cheshire Records Preserved in the Public Record Office, London. Selby. Lancashire and Cheshire Record Society, 1882-83.
Lancashire Glossary. Nodal, Milner. English Dialect Society, 1875-82.
Landnámabók ('Islendinga Sögur'). Kongelige Nordiske Oldskrift Selskab (Copenhagen), 1843.

LIST OF WORKS QUOTED

Liber Vitæ Ecclesiæ Dunelmensis. Stevenson's ed. Surtees Society, 1841.
   do.   Sweet's ed. Early English Text Society, 1885.
Manipulus Vocabulorum. Levin, 1570. Early English Text Society, 1867.
Mediæval Surnames and their Various Spellings. Grazebrook. Society of Antiquaries, 1897.
Memorials of Liverpool. Picton, 1875.
Mersey, Ancient and Modern. Blower, 1878.
Monasticon Anglicanum. Dugdale, 1682; Ellis's ed. 1817-30.
Monumenta Historica Britannica. Petrie, Sharpe, Hardy, 1848.
Moore Charters and Documents Relating to Liverpool: Report to the City Council. Part I. Picton, 1889.
Names and their Histories. Taylor, 1896.
Names, Surnames, and Nic-Names of the Anglo-Saxons. Kemble. Archæological Institute of Great Britain, 1846.
Ninth Inquisitions (Nonarum Inquisitiones).
Notes on English Etymology. Skeat. Philological Society, *passim.*
Oldest English Texts. Sweet. Early English Text Society, 1885.
Patent Rolls (Rotuli Litterarum Patentium).
Pipe Rolls (Magni Rotuli Pipæ).
Place-Names in the Hundred of Wirral. Irvine. Lancashire and Cheshire Historic Society, 1891-92.
Polychronicon Ranulphi Higden Monachi Cestrensis, with Trevisa's and another Translation. Babbington and Lumby's ed., 1865-86.
Portfolio of Fragments relative to the History and Antiquities of Lancashire. Gregson, 1817; Harland's ed., 1869.
Post-Mortem Inquisitions (Calendarium Inquisitionum Post Mortem).
Pre-Norman Sculptured Stones in Lancashire. Browne. Lancashire and Cheshire Antiquarian Society, 1887.
Promptorium Parvulorum. Way's ed. Camden Society, 1843-65.
Proper Names in Philological and Ethnological Enquiries. Picton. Literary and Philosophical Society, Liverpool, 1865-66.
Ptolemy Elucidated. Rylands, 1893.
Rise and Progress of the English Commonwealth: Anglo-Saxon Period. Palgrave, 1832.
Rymer's Fœdera.
Saxonis Grammatici Gesta Danorum. Holder's ed., 1886.
   do.   First nine books translated and edited by Elton and Powell respectively, 1894.
Saxons in England. Kemble. Birch's ed., 1876.
Science of Language. Max Müller, 1862-64.
Scôp or Gleeman's Tale. Thorpe's ed., 1889.
Scottish Land-Names. Maxwell, 1894.
South Lancashire Dialect. Picton. Literary and Philosophical Society, Liverpool, 1864.
Survey of 1320-1346 ('Three Lancashire Documents'). Chetham Society, 1868.
Testa de Nevill.
Traces of History in the Names of Places. Edmunds, 1872.

'Twixt Mersey and Dee. Mrs. Gamlin, 1897.
Village Community. Gomme, 1890.
Words and Places. Taylor, 1864, 1873.

NOTE.—Several treatises quoted are not inserted in the foregoing list owing to their lack of bibliographical interest.

THE PUBLICATIONS OF THE FOLLOWING SOCIETIES ARE QUOTED:

    Archæological Institute of Great Britain.
    Camden Society.
    Chester Archæological Society.
    Chetham Society.
    Early English Text Society.
    English Dialect Society,
    English Historical Society.
    Historic Society of Lancashire and Cheshire.
    Kongelige Nordiske Oldskrift Selskab (Copenhagen).
    Lancashire and Cheshire Antiquarian Society.
    Literary and Philosophical Society of Liverpool.
    Numismatic Society.
    Philological Society.
    Pipe Roll Society.
    Record Society of Lancashire and Cheshire.
    Society of Antiquaries.
    Surtees Society.

THE END.

Elliot Stock, 62, Paternoster Row, London

www.ingramcontent.com/pod-product-compliance
Lightning Source LLC
Chambersburg PA
CBHW020152170426
43199CB00010B/1010